Co-Counselling

The theory behind *Co-Counselling* argues that emotional expression should be welcomed. By taking turns giving and receiving attention, it is possible to recover from past distress, accelerate personal growth and to increase resilience.

This accessible book offers a serious challenge to much of what is currently considered good practice in mental health services. It provides a comprehensive introduction to the basic theory and practice of Co-Counselling as well as its most recent developments, and opens a dialogue between Co-Counselling and other therapeutic approaches. The reader also benefits from inclusion of vignettes outlining the experiences of people from a range of backgrounds offering evidence of the value of Co-Counselling.

Co-Counselling offers a model that has implications for anyone struggling with emotional problems, particularly those facing or recovering from discrimination, prejudice and oppression. Counsellors and psychotherapists will find this book to be an invaluable resource which both challenges and stimulates.

Katie Kauffman is an editor of Co-Counselling publications and teaches Co-Counselling classes.

Caroline New is Senior Lecturer in Sociology at Bath Spa University College and a teacher of Co-Counselling.

Advancing Theory in Therapy
Series Editor: Keith Tudor

Most books covering individual therapeutic approaches are aimed at the trainee/student market. This series, however, is concerned with *advanced* and *advancing* theory, offering the reader comparative and comparable coverage of a number of therapeutic approaches.

Aimed at professionals and postgraduates, *Advancing Theory in Therapy* will cover an impressive range of theories. With full reference to case studies throughout, each title will

- present cutting-edge research findings
- locate each theory and its application within its cultural context
- develop a critical view of theory and practice.

Titles in the series

Body Psychotherapy
Edited by Tree Staunton

Transactional Analysis: A Relational Perspective
Helena Hargaden and Charlotte Sills

Adlerian Psychotherapy: An Advanced Approach to Individual Psychology
Ursula E. Oberst and Alan E. Stewart

Rational Emotive Behaviour Therapy: Theoretical Developments
Edited by Windy Dryden

Co-Counselling: The Theory and Practice of Re-evaluation Counselling
Katie Kauffman and Caroline New

Analytical Psychology
Edited by Joe Cambray and Linda Carter

Co-Counselling

The Theory and Practice of Re-evaluation Counselling

Katie Kauffman and Caroline New

Brunner-Routledge
Taylor & Francis Group

HOVE AND NEW YORK

First published 2004 by Brunner-Routledge
27 Church Road, Hove, East Sussex BN3 2FA

Simultaneously published in the USA and Canada
by Brunner-Routledge
29 West 35th Street, New York NY 10001

Brunner-Routledge is an imprint of the Taylor & Francis Group

© 2004 Katie Kauffman and Caroline New

Typeset in Times by Keystroke, Jacaranda Lodge, Wolverhampton
Printed and bound in Great Britain by MPG Books Ltd, Bodmin
Paperback cover design by Sandra Heath

This publication has been produced with paper manufactured to strict
environmental standards and with pulp derived from sustainable forests.

British Library Cataloguing in Publication Data
A catalogue record for this book is available from the British Library

Library of Congress Cataloging-in-Publication Data
Kauffman, Katie.
  Co-Counselling : the theory and practice of Re-evaluation Counselling /
Katie Kauffman, Caroline New.–1st ed.
    p. ; cm.–(Advancing theory in therapy)
  Includes bibliographical references and index.
  ISBN 1-58391-209-6 (hardcover) – ISBN 1-58391-210-X (pbk.)
  1. Re-evaluation counseling.
  [DNLM: 1. Counseling–methods. WM 55 K21c 2004] I. New, Caroline, 1946–
II. Title. III. Series.

  BF637.C6K3446 2004
  158′.3–dc22   200400456

ISBN 1-58391-209-6 (hbk)
ISBN 1-58391-210-X (pbk)

Contents

Preface   vii
Acknowledgements   viii

Introduction   1

1   A view of human nature   7

2   Human intelligence   19

3   Intermittent and chronic patterns and the inherent human   29

4   The recovery process   41

5   Co-Counselling   52

6   Hurts from oppression   73

7   Stories   90

8   Re-evaluation Counselling in relation to other approaches   116

9   Advancing theory in Re-evaluation Counselling   130

Appendix 1 Working together to end racism   144

Appendix 2 Re-evaluation Counselling publications   149

Appendix 3 How to contact Re-evaluation Counselling   151

References   152
Index   157

Preface

This series focuses on advanced and advancing theory in psychotherapy. Its aims are: to present theory and practice within a specific theoretical orientation or approach at an advanced, postgraduate level; to advance theory by presenting and evaluating new ideas and their relation to the approach; to locate the orientation and its applications within cultural contexts both historically in terms of the origins of the approach and contemporarily in terms of current debates about philosophy, theory, society and therapy; and, finally, to present and develop a critical view of theory and practice, especially in the context of debates about power, organisation and the increasing professionalisation of therapy.

Some readers may be surprised at the inclusion of a volume on Co-Counselling in this series. While Co-Counselling (or Re-evaluation Counselling) is not generally or traditionally regarded as a psychotherapy and, indeed, does not claim to be, it has made and continues to make an important contribution to our understanding of human beings and human situations. Co-Counselling has specific ideas about a range of issues concerning the nature of being human, the impact of being hurt and of social oppression, and reparative contact. Professionals and lay people alike may find some of these ideas challenging; all of them are central to psychotherapeutic endeavour and are of interest to therapists from other theoretical orientations. Harvey Jackins, the founder of Re-evaluation Counselling, also had specific ideas about the nature of theory which influence how Co-Counsellors work and communicate, which, in turn, has informed both the content and presentation of this book. This creatively constructed contribution addresses the brief and concerns of the series, and I am grateful to both authors for their willingness not only to find ways of working together across an ocean and a continent, but also to consult and dialogue with colleagues and reference people within the international Co-Counselling community – and with me as series editor. As the authors themselves acknowledge, Co-Counselling publications have, to date, been largely written and read 'in house', and have not generally been available to a professional therapeutic audience. It is therefore particularly significant and gratifying that this book is appearing in this series and I recommend it, especially to the sceptical reader.

Keith Tudor

Acknowledgements

Our thanks to the anonymous contributors to this book. Your work has enriched the book immeasurably.

Thanks to others who took part in meetings and/or Co-Counselling sessions connected with the book, and offered valuable feedback and encouragement: John Bampfyeld, Ann Bartz, Jim Bottomley, Fenella Butler, Mick Carr, Maria Forsythe, Belinda French, Kevin Geraghty, Sparky Griego, Pommy Harmer, Susan Hutchison, Joan Ostrove, Marion Ouphouet, Ellie Putnam, Pam Roby, Sean Ruth, Samantha Sanderson, Jo Saunders, Janet Sayers, Jayne Schauer, Jenny Spinner and Brian Smeaton.

Thanks to the following who helped in the editing process: Gordon Jackins, Tim Jackins, Lisa Kauffman, Debbie Newton, Marion Ouphouet, Jim Read, Samantha Sanderson, April Sasaki, Diane Shisk, Karen Slaney, Jenny Spinner, Keith Tudor and Dorann Van Heeswyjk, and the rest of the Routledge team.

We particularly thank Samantha Sanderson, Jo Saunders and Dorann Van Heeswyjk for ongoing counselling support and encouragement at crucial moments.

Finally, thanks to friends and family for their consistent support: Stephen Anderson, Anna Freeman, Debbie Freeman, Norman Freeman, Sarah Freeman and Lisa Kauffman.

Introduction

Re-evaluation Counselling (summary statement)

Re-evaluation Counselling (also called RC or Co-Counselling) is a process whereby people of all ages and of all backgrounds can learn how to exchange effective help with each other, in order to free themselves from the effects of past distress experiences.

Re-evaluation Counselling theory provides a model of what a human being can be like in the area of his or her interaction with other human beings and his or her environment. The theory assumes that everyone is born with tremendous intellectual potential, natural zest and lovingness, but that these qualities become blocked and obscured as the result of accumulated distress experiences (fear, hurt, loss, pain, anger, embarrassment and so on) which begin early in our lives.

Any young person would recover from such distress spontaneously by use of the natural process of emotional discharge (crying, trembling, raging, laughing, angry storming, talking, yawning). However, this natural process is usually interfered with by well-meaning people ('Don't cry', 'Be a big boy' and so on), who erroneously equate the emotional discharge (the healing of the hurt) with the hurt itself.

When adequate emotional discharge can take place, the person is freed from the rigid pattern of behaviour and feeling left by the hurt. The basic loving, cooperative, intelligent and enthusiastic nature is then free to operate.

In recovering and using the natural discharge process, two people take turns counselling and being counselled. The one acting as the counsellor listens, draws the other out, and permits, encourages and assists emotional discharge. The one acting as client talks and discharges and re-evaluates. With experience and increased confidence and trust in each other, the process works better and better.*

*This succinct statement describing Re-evaluation Counselling can be found on the back page of each issue of *Present Time* copyright © 2004 Rational Island Publisher. Reproduced with permission of Rational Island Publisher.

A brief history

An accidental happening in Seattle, Washington, USA, in 1950 was the impetus for research which led to the theory outlined above. Harvey Jackins, who later founded RC, agreed to help prevent an acquaintance, Merle, from being committed to a mental hospital. During the next few months Harvy sat with Merle and listened as he cried, shook, and laughed for hours at a time, steadily progressing from an incapacitated state to recovery well beyond any of his previous adult functioning.

Harvey and some others recognised that something profound had occurred, and proceeded to experiment with listening to each other and encouraging emotional discharge. Harvey opened a small office in downtown Seattle and offered counselling under the name of Personal Counselors, Inc.

Harvey and his early associates developed the foundation of the theory by doing many hours of one-way counselling. The same client would often have multiple hours in one day or one week. Harvey built the theory only on what he observed, discarding any previously held assumptions, including those found in other theories of human behaviour.

In 1958, Personal Counselors began to hold classes in 'Personal Re-evaluation Counseling', open to the broader public, taught first by Harvey and later by others whom he had taught. In these classes, people learned how to Co-Counsel – to exchange listening with one another. Classes were held only in Seattle and the surrounding area until about 1970, when the theory and practice spread beyond Seattle.

The Fundamentals of Co-Counseling Manual was published in 1962 (Personal Counselors 1962), soon followed by the first book of RC theory, *The Human Side of Human Beings* (Jackins 1965). In 1973, Harvey's first collection of writings, *The Human Situation*, was published. In 1970, the monthly newsletter of Personal Counselors was replaced by a quarterly journal of the Re-evaluation Counselling Communities, called *Present Time*, which is still published at the present time.

Re-evaluation Counselling first spread beyond Seattle by word of mouth. Then people who had had some Co-Counselling experience began teaching classes, first in California, then on the East Coast of the United States, and then in England. Before long, Harvey, and later other leaders, travelled to many parts of the world leading RC workshops. There is now Co-Counselling activity in ninety-three countries.

As the number of participants in Co-Counselling increased, there emerged a need for an organisational structure that would support growth while keeping the theory and practice of RC accurate. A means of certifying teachers was developed, and basic agreements for organising RC classes (and later, the RC Communities) were established.

As RC spread beyond English-speaking countries, basic materials began to be translated by volunteers. Audio and videotapes were also produced to facilitate the teaching of RC theory.

In the spring of 1975, in Pennsylvania, USA, Co-Counsellors of African, Asian, Latino/a, Jewish and Native American heritage caucused to explore the implications of RC theory and practice for their constituencies, then reported to the entire workshop. Men and women also met in separate groups to consider the implications for their genders, and reported back to the larger group. RC theory and practice were found to be useful in the recovery from hurtful experiences specific to each group, and to 'oppressed' groups in general (Jackins *et al.* 1976).

When Harvey Jackins died in July 1999, Tim Jackins (his son), who had been the Alternate International Reference Person, became the International Reference Person. Diane Shisk was appointed Alternate International Reference Person. Under Tim's and Diane's leadership, the Re-evaluation Counselling Communities have continued in the directions already set in the earlier decades, as well as expanding into some new areas.

This book

Re-evaluation Counselling and its development have particular features that have influenced our presentation of it. In general, RC has not been communicated to others as part of an academic discipline or professional training. It has made few appearances in universities or in dialogues among students of counselling or psychotherapy. One reason for this is that our publications have been written by and primarily for Co-Counsellors and are mostly read 'in house'. Information about Re-evaluation Counselling has not, in general, been available to therapists or to the general public. RC policy from early on has been to involve people only to the extent we have accumulated sufficient human resources (of attention and skill) to teach and support each person well. Until recently it has seemed that widespread publicity might overwhelm these resources.

People have usually found out about Co-Counselling from friends. Then they have learnt more formally in fundamentals classes. We – the authors – are Co-Counsellors and teachers of Co-Counselling. We are best prepared to explain Re-evaluation Counselling as it is usually communicated and as we ourselves have taught it in Fundamentals of Co-Counselling classes. For this reason, we have tried to approximate with the written word what happens in a class. One way has been to include Co-Counsellors in the book as 'class members'. You will also notice our encouragement to you, the reader, to try out these ideas and practices as we go along. We think the resulting book accurately portrays Re-evaluation Counselling, both in our description of the theory and practice and in these other aspects of the presentation.

Chapters 8 and 9 discuss 'advancing theory' in RC, and relate RC to major therapeutic approaches. It has made sense to present this material in a more formal style. We hope the two styles (in the first seven chapters of the book, and in the last two) will complement each other and meet the needs of a variety of readers.

As we do in a typical Co-Counselling class, we will now begin with intro-ductions. (All the contributors to this book, with the exception of the authors, are using pseudonyms.)

I'm **Katie Kauffman**, co-author of this book. I've been participating in Re-evaluation Counselling for thirty-six years – since 1968 – and am pleased to share what I know about it. Since 1972, I've worked at Personal Counselors, Inc. in Seattle, where Re-evaluation Counselling theory was researched and developed. I also work for the publishing arm of Re-evaluation Counselling, Rational Island Publishers, as editor and producer of publications about Re-evaluation Counselling. I'm a 61-year-old white woman and have lived in Seattle all my life. Before working at Personal Counselors and Rational Island Publishers, I worked as an elementary school teacher, playground supervisor, secretary and teacher of English in Japan. I've a master's degree in China Studies and have travelled to China twice, the first time in 1975. I enjoy being with my family and friends, watercolour and pastel painting, gardening, neighbourhood organising, and working for social change.

I'm **Caroline New**, co-author of this book. I've been Co-Counselling for twenty-two years. I'm a white woman, born in Wales, to English parents, just after the war. Both my grandfathers were skilled workers, my father was a telephone engineer who worked his way into a non-manual job, and my mother was a teacher. I live in England with my husband – we've been together for over thirty years now and we have a lot of fun. My husband's parents were refugees from Warsaw, and I was close to them until their deaths a few years ago. We have three grown-up daughters. In one way or another I've been an activist for social change all of my adult life. I believe in the possibility of a world organised to treat all human beings well, and to meet human needs in a way that respects our environment. I used to enjoy rock-climbing. I can't do that any more but I still love walking in hills and mountains, or along the coast. Luckily, I like writing and I am pleased to have this chance to tell people about something that's made a big difference to my own life.

I'm **Emma**. I'm a white woman, aged 40. I became disabled in 1991, just about a year after I started in RC. I have very poor health. The future I had mapped out for myself changed dramatically. I now spend a lot of time fighting with social services about home care and filling in benefits forms. RC has helped me enormously to keep rethinking what I want from my life, especially to push hard against all the misinformation I am fed everyday about how tragic it is to be a disabled person. I have a completely different life to what I would have had if I did not have this amazing tool. As for other aspects of my life, when I've got time, I talk to friends all over the world on the Internet. I like writing, and I like some science-fiction television shows, when they are well scripted. I have an asthmatic cat, and I've done research into feline asthma.

I'm **Gillian**. I am a white woman, 41 years old, with two children (14 and 9).

I was raised working class. I'm married to someone who is self-employed. He tries not to work in the holidays so we have time together with the children, and I've made a decision not to work full time. I do some paid work, youth work and some voluntary work in my village, and make time to see friends and family. I'm currently working on singing semi-professionally. I've spent much of my life doing what other people want me to do, but the singing is just for me – nobody's told me to do it. I have been using Co-Counselling for about fourteen years. I started a Re-evaluation Counselling playgroup nearly seven years ago which ran for four years.

My name is **Kerry**. I'm a single father of a 19-year-old daughter. I was born in Northern Ireland, and live in England now. I've been using Co-Counselling for about fifteen years. I work in the city council three days a week in the Housing Benefits department. I enjoy drawing, especially cartooning, and I'm active in the British small press. I have two sisters and a brother. I'm especially close to my younger sister, who lives near me, and she was the reason I originally came to live here seventeen years ago. I enjoy being an uncle to my nephew and niece.

My name is **Daire** [which is a guy's name, and pronounced 'Dara']. I'm 18 years old, and from Dublin, Ireland. At time of writing I'm approaching my Leaving Certificate exams (high school finals). Much as I would like to give some kind of introduction or description of myself, it's been so long since I haven't been bogged down in studying for the exams that I only have a vague recollection of my life outside of school. I'm the middle child in a family of five from a middle-class suburb of Dublin. I'm looking to study engineering this coming autumn, but ideally (although this is possibly a little fanciful) I'd like to get into pyrotechnics, or else sit in a big room full of Lego all day long, and design the new models. I was a Catholic for the first fifteen years of my life, before becoming what one might call a born-again Christian. That dominated the next two years of my life, although since that time I have considered myself an atheist. I first entered Re-evaluation Counselling when my father, who has been involved since the 1970s, taught a fundamentals class at our house. It was tough at times, to begin with, but I was always fascinated with the theory. So I stuck around, mainly to hear that, and I'm still here now, a little over three years later.

Neil: I was born in Belfast in Northern Ireland in a traditional working-class Protestant Unionist family. Part of me loves my heritage and my people, and part of me is deeply ashamed of some of the things we've done. I was 14 when the 'Troubles' started, and I left Belfast when I was 24 and moved to England. I like living in England, but Belfast is my home – much as I hate it. I came out as Gay in Belfast and was working with a group to force the British government to change the law in Northern Ireland. At that time homosexuality was completely illegal in Northern Ireland, and we took the case to the European Court of Human Rights and won. I've been involved with RC for about eighteen years. RC has been the place where I have been able to be most myself as a Gay Protestant Northern Irish man. It's been a safe place for me to look at my different identities and what they mean to me. Various things happened in my life, and I decided I wanted to be in a relationship with a woman and have children. I now live with my wife and our two young children. I love being a father. Growing up as a Protestant in Northern Ireland there wasn't much room for feelings, but music was a key place where I was able to feel things. I love Joni Mitchell, and recently I've discovered country blue-grass. Matisse is one of my favourite painters, and a high spot of my life was going to New York in 2000 to see the Matisse exhibition.

Ebony: I am an African-heritage woman. I was born in a small rural community in south Georgia, USA. I grew up there with six sisters and my parents on a small family farm. I was the first in my generation to go to college and attended college in Atlanta, Georgia. Right after college I ended up in New York City because of a summer job and stayed for the next thirty-two years. I'm now 56 and live on the West Coast of the USA. I've been using Co-Counselling for twelve years and absolutely love it and the differences it has made in my life. I could spend hours talking about its importance to me, but you can begin trying it out while reading this book, and that is most important, as you must experience the process for it to be most meaningful.

Rachael: I'm a middle-aged Jewish woman, married, with two young children, and the focus of my life at this point is Co-Counselling, leading in Co-Counselling and raising my children. I began Co-Counselling when I was 22. Earlier in my life I worked in the legislative and executive branches of government, in television and in social change organisations.

Jenny: I'm a 48-year-old white woman. I have been Co-Counselling since I was 17. I taught my first Co-Counselling class when I was 19. My interests these days are helping to build community in my neighbourhood, Co-Counselling, and working for social change. I was involved in anti-nuclear-war events, worked on a couple of presidential campaigns, and am currently involved with local peace and justice activities. I've worked temporarily as a waitress, cannery worker, fundraiser, and manager of a small fast-food restaurant. I went to medical school and did a year of internship and currently work as an editor.

Having convened our class, we are now ready to talk about the core theory of Re-evaluation Counselling.

Chapter 1

A view of human nature

Vast intelligence, zestful enjoyment of living, loving, co-operative relationships with others – these seem to constitute the essential human nature.

(Jackins 1965: 28)

Our basic nature

The first assumption we will talk about concerns our basic nature as human beings
(Jackins 1965). We assume that humans are highly intelligent, good, cooperative,
loving, enthusiastic, hopeful, responsible, powerful (and many other positive
characteristics).

It is not part of our inherent nature to hurt others, to be defeated by problems or
to make the same mistakes over and over again, to fail to enjoy life, to have
conflicts with others, to be unable to take charge or initiate needed changes, or to
dislike or hate others or ourselves. As we will see, these negative characteristics
are the result of having been hurt.

We find that assuming a good basic human nature is a key element in effective
counselling. This assumption leads to many more useful and interesting con-
clusions than the opposite view. With the theory of Re-evaluation Counselling
to guide us – with confidence in the intelligence and goodness of every person –
we have a basis for being delighted with and confident for others, and ourselves.
We have a basis for questioning and rejecting any negative or hopeless judgements
about people.

We have heard many despairing messages about human nature and human
prospects, but in fact we humans are basically hopeful. Even in difficult circumstances, we continue searching for hopeful, positive, useful perspectives on our
personal existence and that of the human species.

We are intelligent

We define intelligence as the ability to come up with a fresh, accurate response to
each moment of living. Human intelligence operates by receiving new information
from the environment, by comparing and contrasting this new information with

information from past experiences that have already been understood and stored in the memory, and by constructing a fresh, new, appropriate response to the specific situation at hand. We begin life with a huge amount of this ability. (Being intelligent is not the same as knowing a lot – this confusion often leads people to belittle the great intelligence of young people.)

Our complex nervous system has thousands of billions of separate nerve cells that communicate with each other in an enormous number of ways. We can meet each new situation with a completely new response that we have created, just that moment, exactly to handle that situation. As we get information from our surroundings and our interactions with it, we can keep modifying what we are doing and become more and more successful as we continue to operate. Current brain research also supports the claim that human capacities are far greater than that reflected in the levels of functioning we normally achieve (Ramachandran and Blakeslee 1998).

We know of people who excel at several complex careers in a lifetime, people who are acclaimed as geniuses. Many people can speak several languages *and* practise a physical skill to a high level *and* think well about the people they love. However, even these people are using only a fraction of the capacities of their immensely flexible brains.

Our understanding of intelligence – what it is, how huge it is, how it works under optimum conditions, how hurts interfere with it, and how we can recover it fully – is at the centre of this theory and practice.[1]

We are good

Unhurt human beings are intelligently kind, compassionate, cooperative, caring of their environment and committed to justice. Humans inherently want things to be right for everyone and everything. Our goodness is an aspect of our intelligence. It is independent of what we do or accomplish, and it continues to exist even if we do things that are irrational and destructive. All of us show great courage, persistence and inventiveness as we strive to live and live well. We do everything we can think of to have good lives, and we want other people to thrive, too. When we see someone in distress, we want to help and we assist to the best of our ability. We participate in organisations and political movements for the purpose of good. We seek religious and philosophical frameworks to help us live well. We try hard to enjoy life; we take any opportunity to have fun and be playful. We are brave, caring, tenacious survivors. We are good.

We enjoy closeness and cooperation with other humans

We are social beings and interdependent, closely connected to each other and to all other living things. We are also connected to the non-living entities and processes of our environment. Our minds find other human minds deeply enjoyable, interesting and attractive. We inherently seek closeness with other people and communication with them. Closeness and cooperation come naturally to us and enhance our survival.

We are loving

Love is the way we human beings naturally feel about each other and is another aspect of our intelligence. We need to be loved, and to love.[2]

We enjoy life; we are zestful

Enthusiastic enjoyment of life is our natural tone. We are eager to learn and to enjoy all that is going on around us. Young people often show this characteristic clearly; they are eager to experience all that a new day offers. 'Let's go!'

We are responsible

We have a natural attitude of responsibility for everything. This attitude is relaxed and eager. Rational responsibility is not a heavy burden or the same as obligation. Responsibility means we can make everything we touch flourish and be right! We have the freedom to take charge. When something needs to be made right, improved or enhanced, an unhurt human will notice it, think about it and act. We enjoy taking leadership. Unless we have been made confused by distress, we don't take responsibility in isolation; we find ways to attract others to worthy projects and lead and organise group efforts.

We are powerful

We have the ability to make the universe respond to us as we wish it to. It may take a long time, a lot of effort and the cooperation of other humans, but what we rationally want to accomplish can be accomplished. (This is not how we've been taught to think about power – as power 'over' someone, power to push people around.)

No matter what happened in the past, we are not limited by it. We are not limited to distressed perspectives or doomed to repeat destructive actions. When we have access to our intelligence, human power to bring about change is enormous.

Babies are powerful. They use their powerful voices to get attention and action.

> In a rational environment that voice alone would be enough to see that prompt action is taken to carry out the child's wishes. The intuitive feeling a child has of being in charge should correspond to reality.
>
> (Jackins 1978a: 96)

We are hopeful

Humans begin life hopeful. And we stay hopeful – about our own prospects and about the prospects for all humans – even under difficult conditions. Feelings of hopelessness, discouragement, cynicism, isolation, despair and so on are the result of hurt, not of our inherent nature.

We are all very much alike

We are all members of the same sub-species and closely related. Our physical differences are trivial compared to all that we have in common. There is no rational basis for the many ways we have been separated from each other – for example, by racism, sexism and ageism – that have claimed justification on the grounds of physical differences.

We naturally give and receive attention

We are all fully equipped to help others recover from distresses and to use the natural healing process for our own recovery. It is basic to us to be a 'counsellor' and a 'client'.

We are wonderful in many additional ways

All of us – of whatever gender, class, race, nationality, age or any other grouping we can think of – are inherently courageous, gentle, sensitive, strong, beautiful, creative, tender, generous, decisive, energetic, open, trusting, trustworthy, playful, hopeful and much more.

We fit well with our benign world and universe

Our world and universe are supportive of our survival and functioning. Everything we require for meeting our needs exists in the universe. Times of good close contact with others, with our own and others' goodness and intelligence, and with the wonder and beauty of the world are glimpses of how life can be when we are in touch with our inherent human nature.

Being hurt

If human beings are basically good and intelligent, what happens to make us so prone to unintelligent behaviour and a whole host of negative feelings? We see people hurting others and themselves, being uncooperative and feeling unhappy. We see relationships fraught with conflict, among individuals, groups and nations. We see the destruction of the environment on which all life depends. We see a world in recurrent crisis because of irrational social organisation and irrational individual and group action.

Re-evaluation Counselling theory explains the difference between our inherent natures and our poor functioning in a simple way: we get hurt. Loved ones die, people are injured or get sick, storms devastate farms and ships sink. Some hurts we experience depend on unique individual circumstances – for example, where we happen to have been born, who looked after us, and the hurts our caretakers themselves have suffered.

We get hurt early in our lives. As infants we depend on adults to meet our needs. It is hurtful when we do not get the physical care, love and attention we need. It hurts if we are not delighted in and valued as unique beings. When the adults around us are irrational, we have little recourse. Our lack of experience makes it impossible to put what is happening to us in context (a good thing about growing older is that we accumulate information which we can use to understand what is happening around us).

Distress is contagious: when one person has been hurt, the way that he or she is affected has an effect on others. Parents and other adults greatly influence us when we are young and dependent on them. Under present and past social conditions, adults have inevitably passed on to new humans at least some of the ways they were hurt. Adults unwittingly act out on young people the mistreatment they once received. (We describe how this may happen in the next chapter.)

Without intending to, our caretakers have also passed on much cultural misinformation. For example, there is the idea that some people are just 'bad'. There are ubiquitous messages that reinforce powerlessness – 'That's just how things are, and the sooner you get used to it the better', or, in response to youthful optimism and exuberance, 'Just wait until you grow up – *you'll* see (what life is *really* like)'. In the grip of their fears, our caretakers may have told us lies about people different from ourselves – even though they never meant to misinform us.

A source of enormous hurt is social *oppression* – the systematic institutionalised mistreatment of people because they belong to a particular group: racism, classism, sexism, ageism, Gay oppression, anti-Semitism and the many other 'isms'. Humans also suffer from injustice, starvation, epidemics, massacres, war, genocide and other catastrophes caused by the poor functioning of social and political systems. We describe the effects of oppression and internalised oppression in Chapter 6.

In general, humans have not had the opportunity to significantly notice our hurts, their extent and how damaging they are. There hasn't been a supportive enough context or enough time to really look at them.

Unless we have the opportunity to recover, hurts stay with us and affect us. We don't feel and function as well as we did before we were hurt. We can't think as well. We may not feel and act as lovable and loving. We may feel insecure instead of confident. We feel bad a lot of the time. We unthinkingly pass on to others the mistreatment we've endured. We may hate and fear people who are different from us. When we are in a position of power, we may use it to further our own interests at the expense of others. Or we may be unable to get what is rightfully ours because we feel powerless and hopeless. We describe how accumulated hurts affect us in Chapter 3.

An invitation to try Co-Counselling

In a typical Co-Counselling class, and therefore in this book, we do not talk (or write) for very long without giving the class (and you the reader) the opportunity to be an active participant. At this point we invite you to get some hands-on experience. You will need a partner. This is an opportunity to both listen and be listened to, about anything at all. If you need a focus, you might tell how your day has gone so far. How are you feeling? What has gone well today? Have there been any little or big upsets?

Everyone is familiar with talking and listening. What people often experience as a startling new experience is *taking turns* doing this. A Co-Counselling session is two people taking turns listening and paying attention to each other.

For this first 'mini-session', when you are the listener (in the counsellor role), please try an experiment – do not say anything. A Co-Counselling session has a different purpose from a conversation, and it's good to put the brakes on our accustomed mode of relating to others from the very start. You'll get to notice what it is like to focus your full attention on someone without having to work out what to say. You'll be freer to notice not only what your partner is saying, but also his or her facial expression, posture and tone of voice – all of which will be communicating something. At the same time, keep eye contact and show interest and warmth with your face.

When you are being listened to (in the 'client' role), feel free to talk about whatever is on your mind, and also, since most of us aren't used to being listened to without any interaction, notice what that feels like and any other feelings that arise.

Set a timer, if you have one, and after two minutes, exchange roles.

In a typical Co-Counselling class participants are invited to share their impressions of the short session. People often say it was difficult not to say anything as the listener and that it felt odd not to be conversing. Others have wanted to ask questions to satisfy their curiosity. Some have found it hard to hold back their reactions to what was being said. They are noticing some of the impulses that, if acted upon, will not be useful in Co-Counselling sessions.

At the same time, people often notice they feel freer to pay good attention because they don't have to focus on what they might say. They feel relieved not to have to scramble mentally to solve the client's problems. (They are sometimes puzzled and wonder if they will ever get to be more active as counsellor. We reassure them that they will.)

People sometimes say that as 'client', they enjoyed the undivided attention. Sometimes people find it hard to think of what to say as clients. Sometimes they feel uncomfortable having someone look directly at them without interacting in the usual ways. Sometimes they feel embarrassed or even fearful. For an occasional person, it's as if he or she has been eagerly waiting for a chance to pour out thoughts and feelings. It will be different for each person.

Having had this chance to do a short session, and as we talk about it afterward, class members get to know each other a little and usually feel more at ease. This makes it easier to take in information. We might have everyone do another short session with someone else, to keep breaking the ice, and maybe another, and another. By this time people are usually having a good time and feel in closer contact with each other.

If you tried it, what was it like for you? Could you keep from talking when you were the listener? What thoughts went through your mind that you felt like saying? As the client, did you enjoy being listened to without interruption? (If you liked doing this, you might want to pursue taking equal turns listening and talking with your friends and family. It need not be for the purpose of solving problems, emotional or otherwise. It can just be an enjoyable time giving full attention to someone else's thoughts, and for you to be heard, too.)

Here are some questions related to the theory presentation: in what ways do you think well? Do you know that you are good? Loving? Can you remember times you felt deep caring for another person? Can you remember a time you enjoyed someone's mind? Your own mind? Under what conditions do you feel especially enthusiastic and alive? Have you enjoyed responsibility? Do you remember feeling hopeful? Have you noticed your power? What experiences have you had of knowing that people, or the world we live in, are excellent and benign? (Exchanging listening with someone can make it easier to think about these questions.)

Our class for the purposes of this book is different from a fundamentals class in that the participants are experienced Co-Counsellors. Therefore, rather than focus on this first short session, they will share more generally about their early Co-Counselling experiences, as well as comment on the theory topic.

Experience-sharing

Neil: I enjoyed Co-Counselling from the start – it was such a relief to talk to someone who was really listening. It was great to be part of a small group of people who didn't know each other and slowly showed more and more of themselves until by the end we trusted each other a lot and were very loving with each other. A friend invited me to an introductory lecture, and toward the end the teacher counselled him in front of the group. This made me feel uncomfortable and embarrassed, especially when he got upset. When it came to questions, I asked the teacher why he had asked such personal questions and upset my friend. The teacher asked me to come up in front of the group and talk about why it had bothered me. I burst into tears and cried non-stop for fifteen minutes. After that I was hooked. I definitely wanted to find out more about this thing.

Ebony: I'll tell you my first encounter with RC. I belonged to a black women's national health organisation that sought to empower black women about their health. Women organised in neighbourhood support groups and talked about their issues. The leader of the New York City organisation brought in someone to teach the members listening skills. This trainer knew Co-Counselling and taught us a fundamentals class. The first assignment changed my life. We paired up and arranged a listening session outside of class. I talked to this woman who, like me, had been asked to listen with respect, without judgement or comment. Then I listened to her. By the time I arrived back in my apartment, I thought, this is what I've been waiting for all my life. I remembered what the leader had said in class about this process being aimed at reclaiming one's intelligence. After being listened to and understanding that I was OK, that the bad way I felt did not have to be there always, and that I could assist with that change instead of just getting through life, I felt more in charge, felt more hope.

I set about trying to find a class taught by a black person and eventually found a teacher who was about to give an introductory talk. It was on Martin Luther King's (MLK's) birthday. I hesitated about going, thinking I really should be doing something for MLK's birthday. But I went with a friend of mine who was also in this organisation and interested in RC. It was the most important thing I had ever done for my life, and I now know I was indeed doing something for MLK's birthday. I was starting a process that would give me a means to get rid of the internalised messages of racism and other 'isms' that had made me feel and act marginal, worry about not being smart, and feel bad about myself. I had started the process of liberating my mind and being in charge, that has continued to this day. What could be a more powerful tribute to Dr King and what he wanted for black people?

Kerry: For most of my first series of Fundamentals classes, I just laughed and laughed whenever I was given attention.

I remember something that happened before I started using Co-Counselling that I thought about differently once I heard RC's view of the basic goodness of people. I was working in a night shelter, and I was in the office with a couple of women I worked with who suddenly started looking very frightened. I turned round, and one of the men using the shelter was coming in with a wild expression on his face and his arms raised. Even though I'd experienced quite a lot of violence in my upbringing in Northern Ireland, and I was usually ready for a fight, for some reason I turned around that day, took a couple of steps toward him, and put my arms round him. I laid my head on his chest (he was a bigger man than me). There was a pause, and then he started patting me on the back, smiling, and telling me what a good feller I was. He wasn't quite crying, but his eyes filled up, and we just chatted a bit. It was clear to me that I'd called him back from something he didn't want to do, a situation in which people could easily have been hurt. At the time I was more puzzled by my own behaviour than by his reaction. When I came across the Co-Counselling model and the whole idea about inherent goodness, it came to me that what had happened was that I'd been taken off guard sufficiently that part of my inherent self came through in a wonderful way.

Gillian: Having someone listen and not give advice or offer a solution was new to me!

When I think of people and life being good, I think of my daughter's birth, which was a wonderful experience after a difficult time with the birth of my son. I set it up to have lots of support, and I managed a birth free of anaesthesia and with no complications. I was ecstatic!

Jenny: When I was 17, a lot of feelings came up for me all at once. I thought I was mentally 'ill' and initially consulted some professionals. My family was kind, but my sister, who had been in Co-Counselling for several years, seemed to be the only person who really understood what was going on. She told me that I was fine, that there was a good reason why I was feeling bad, and that it was just right to cry a lot. For about six months she would listen and I would cry, nearly every day. I didn't feel any better for those six months, but then the cloud lifted and I felt like I was again the person I had been as a young child. I felt great! Then I started laughing a lot. It was at this point that I joined a Co-Counselling class, and every single bit of the theory I learned there made sense to me because I had experienced it.

I notice how different I, and other people, are after Co-Counselling sessions. Often all I need to do to let go of painful feelings is to notice that I am with another person who is completely human underneath anything I find difficult, and who loves me because that's the way people naturally feel about each other. I can also cry by myself, thinking about people I am close to and getting in touch with how human they are, how I love them and they love me.

Being constantly hurt is so ongoing in this society that it's considered 'normal' and we are numb to it. I think any time we are treated as less than wonderful, and completely respected and loved, it's hurtful, so we're being constantly hurt. I meet many people who say, 'I had a great childhood; I'm fine', but they look like wrecks to me. We've just come to accept that horrible is 'normal'. It's only when someone gets overwhelmed by old feelings that we think they need help.

Rachael: I first heard about Co-Counselling a year after I graduated from college, from my former college roommates who spoke very highly of it. I thought it was a load of nonsense. They gave me a pamphlet called *The Complete Appreciation of Oneself*. I intended never to read it since it looked so 'alternative' but I had a long flight back from California (where they lived) to Washington, DC (where I lived), and I opened the pamphlet. The first instruction in the pamphlet was to go stand in front of a mirror and say something nice about yourself. Since I had time on my hands, I went to the airplane bathroom, looked in the mirror, and couldn't think of anything nice about myself that I really believed. I thought, 'Oops! Something's wrong here!' and I joined a Fundamentals of Co-Counselling class as soon as I got back to DC.

As for the goodness of people and the world, sometimes when my children and I are all cuddled up together in bed at night, I think, 'What a wonderful world to have access to each other like this.'

Daire: As mentioned earlier, when I was 15, I joined a fundamentals class that my father was teaching, out of curiosity supported by convenience – it was held in my living room. I was immediately fascinated by the theory of inherent human nature, which seemed, once I heard it, so obvious, and yet which never would have occurred to me had nobody said it. The counselling itself took somewhat more getting used to. I was quite bogged down at first in wondering what to say and how to look (as counsellor).

Katie: By the time I was 26 I was feeling anxious and depressed all the time. I had seen psychologists, psychiatrists and social workers. They listened and were kind, but I was still confused and miserable. Fortunately, I found my way to Re-evaluation Counselling. It was a long and bumpy road, but with the theory, the discharge process, caring people to assist me, and persistence, by now I've mostly recovered from the early hurt that was at the root of my distressed feelings. Instead of living out life as a 'mental patient', I regained confidence in myself and am doing and enjoying things I would not have imagined were possible.

I don't think I've ever really doubted, deep down, that people are good, that it's good to be alive, and that things are fundamentally fine – although life has certainly seemed awful in the midst of awful feelings. I've been dependably able to notice life's goodness through the natural world, especially the mountains. As a child, I could look out on the mountains from my window. Also, my parents liked to ski and hike, and from the time we were young children, they took us along. They were full of the enjoyment of life when they were out there – and I think that was passed on to me. I'm also inspired by good thinking wherever I've noticed it – the precise words of writers and poets; the clear, on-target communication of young people; the brilliant practical thinking of mechanics; my own creativity, as a poem or drawing pops out from my mind; problem-solving in a group of people when ideas and creativity and fun are bubbling.

Caroline: I began Co-Counselling when I was feeling depressed and needy after the birth of my third baby, despite my delight in her. It helped me take charge of my life. That, and two things, kept me doing it. One was that it was so interesting and moving to hear what went on for other people. The other was the insight it offered about how people get hurt through oppression. My parents were working-class people who became middle-class. This affected my whole childhood, and for the first time ever I began to understand why.

I think the experiences that mean most to us are often those that show us a different view of the world from the distorted picture caused by our hurts, and for me a main hurt was isolation. When I was a child in school I invented a game of shops. The shops sold flowers, which we stole on the way to school. The walls of the shops were made of grass, which we picked in handfuls in the playing field. Grass was also the currency. We sat in the shops or made visits to others' shops and sold the flowers to each other. In my memory we played this game over a whole summer. I was usually a lonely child, but we all played it together, and I was in a state of bliss.

Emma: You ask about times we experienced the world as good. Something happened to me a few years ago that helped me notice my connection to people and the joy of being alive. It was a 'near death experience'. For me, it wasn't like other people describe it. There weren't any bright lights or tunnels or anything like that. I was very ill in hospital, had been having a severe asthma attack for a few days and had pneumonia. I just couldn't take one more painful breath, so I stopped breathing. I remember looking at my watch and seeing the second hand go round once, then twice; then I got a bit worried, and a few alarms went off, and people started coming at me, so I breathed again. (I know now that I was on such a high concentration of oxygen that my body could tolerate my not breathing for a few minutes.) I felt suffused with love – for me, for the world, and for everyone in it. I felt totally at one with the world, safe, loved, and connected to everyone. To know that I could achieve such a feeling of peace, that it was within me to draw upon, was a major breakthrough for me. From then on, I've remained convinced that that awareness I had back then, and have had glimpses of since, is what I'm aiming for in my life.

I'll say something about how we can be trained to push down our feelings. As a child, I lost two grandfathers and a cherished uncle all in a year. I wasn't allowed to grieve – from early on I had been especially hurt around crying. By the time I was in my teens I couldn't react to anything; my family all believed I was 'hard' because I refused to show any emotion. Occasionally, in the middle of the night usually, I'd suddenly become overwhelmed with pain and grief, but I'd hold my breath and make it go away.

Notes

1   RC's notion of intelligence as including and integrating many human functions that are usually treated separately has some affinity with Howard Gardner's multidimensional theory of intelligence (see Gardner 1993).

2   There seems to be a continuing rational inherent need to be loved . . . We need to feel loved, we need to . . . feel that there is some human somewhere who has, at least potentially, this loving attitude toward us. Now this need is widely celebrated and we are not breaking any new paths in saying this. What I think we do need to say, and clearly, is that far more important than the need to be loved is the need to love. You can get along without being loved over long periods of time if necessary, but if you have allowed your outlet of loving others to be sealed then you are in trouble, you are in real trouble.

(Jackins 1978b: 123)

Chapter 2

Human intelligence

Apparently if any of us could preserve in operating condition a very large portion of the flexible intelligence that each of us possesses inherently, the one who did so would be accurately described as an 'all-round genius' by the current standards of our culture.

(Jackins 1965:19)

How our intelligence works

As we have noted previously, human beings begin life with a very large amount of intelligence. We are defining intelligence in a particular way – as the ability to come up with new, flexible, precisely accurate responses to each new moment of living. No two situations are exactly identical, and therefore the ability to respond flexibly and precisely has great survival value.

This ability can be distinguished from the intelligence of most other creatures. Their behaviour is dominated by pre-set patterns of response and rigid conditioning. (A few of the most complex creatures do have some ability to create new responses.)

We can pause at this point to note the uniqueness of our definition of intelligence. People are not used to thinking about it this way. For example, many of us have assumed that young people's lack of information is equivalent to lack of intelligence. Also, we have not in general connected human malfunctioning to an inability to *think*.

This definition of intelligence – and additional assumptions about how human intelligence either remains unencumbered and flexible, or becomes burdened with distress and inflexible – is at the centre of RC theory and practice. The recovery of intelligence from distress is the essence of this practice.

Intelligence under optimum conditions

Our intelligence works in one way when we are relaxed and free from distress. It works in another, different way when we are undergoing a distressing experience.

Let's take the first case, when nothing upsetting is happening.

By means of our sensory channels we perceive a huge volume of sights, sounds, smells, tastes and movements, every moment of our waking lives. Most of this information input is taking place below the level of awareness. We do not awarely notice everything within our field of vision every moment, or all the background sounds, or the smells, or what our sense of touch is conveying to our minds.

In addition, we are interacting with our environment at every moment. We are responding in some way, even if it is resting peacefully. Sometimes we are conscious of solving problems – thinking carefully about a complicated inter-action, for example, or learning a new concept or technical procedure. Maybe we're new at a job and are conscious of trying to respond accurately to the new people we're meeting, the boss and the unfamiliar office procedures. But whether we're conscious of thinking or not, we are continually coming up with responses to whatever situation we are in.

If we want to handle a highly complex negotiation between two antagonists, or to build a bridge, or to end prejudice and bring world peace, we certainly need our minds to function flexibly and precisely. We also need information – some of which will already have been stored in our memory, together with the requisite skills to acquire more – to solve these problems. What has been the background to the negotiation? What mathematical and engineering theory and skills are needed to design the bridge? What understanding of cultural differences, history and politics will we need to figure out how the world's peoples can come to an agreement and cooperate?

We are constantly taking in and processing information, which our mind uses to construct responses. It seems to work as follows. We notice the relevant aspects of the new situation and (instantaneously, in the more familiar situations) draw upon the information stored in our memory to determine how this situation is similar to past ones. Then we form a basis on which to construct our response. At the same time, we note all the ways in which this situation is different from situations we have already understood – and there always are differences because there are no identities in the universe. Certainly billions of factors exist in anything as complicated as the situations that confront human beings.

It might seem, for example, that cooking scrambled eggs today is exactly the same as cooking them yesterday. However, there are many differences. It might be that the small fracture on one of the egg shells means we have to crack the egg a little to the side of that crack, or the shell might collapse in on itself, spilling off to the side of the bowl and giving us a messy clean-up job. Or perhaps there are extra people to breakfast today, so we need to think about how many eggs there are and whether we can dilute them with a little milk to make them go further. We do know, from past experience, the basics of scrambling eggs – we easily pull the saucepan from the cupboard, turn on the burner, put some butter in the pan, crack the eggs in the bowl, stir the eggs with a spoon while letting them cook, and so on. With this as a basis, our intelligence then distinguishes the new factors in today's egg scramble, and we respond, taking those into account.

Over and over, in billions of ways, we move through our days taking in the information around us, relating it to what we already know, and begin to construct a response, while tailor-making that response to fit this unique situation.

As we go, we keep adding to our store of information. These items of information are stored in our memory in discrete (distinct and separable) bits and are available to us that way. We can remember, as needed, any particular detail of the experience. The more experiences we have, the more information we have on file and the more we can do. We can handle more situations. We can solve complex problems that require lots of information. We do this easily when all is going well (see Jackins 1965 for a fuller discussion).

Intelligence under distressed conditions

However, our intelligence does not sort incoming information well when we are hurting and upset. In other words, it's difficult to think when we're in distress. There are common sayings that describe this: 'She walked around in a fog after her mother died.' 'They were scared out of their wits.' 'He was so mad he couldn't hit the ground with his hat.'

When we are hurting, the functioning of our complex, flexible intelligence tends to be interrupted and we struggle to think at all. We tend to revert to acting on the basis of feelings instead of logical thought. We continue to take in all the sights and sounds and tastes and smells and characters and conversations and temperatures and pressures, *but*, with our great computing ability suspended, we relapse to operating on a more primitive kind of functioning. The information input mis-stores. All the many aspects of this experience do not get filed in discrete bits in our memory. With our intelligence suspended, we are not able to compare and contrast these new data with what we already know. The sights, sounds, smells and movements, along with the feelings of distress, are taken in but are all jumbled together in an undifferentiated 'lump'. If we remember anything at all about this accumulation of painful experiences, the tied-together lump of mis-stored information floods our mind, all at once. We can't recall and make use of specific details because they weren't stored that way. They are all mixed together, along with the upset feelings. When this happens, we experience great difficulty in thinking clearly.

Distress recordings (distress patterns)

This lump of mis-stored information has an additional characteristic. It tends to become a rigid recording of the distressful event. In a particular area of our minds, a recording – of a jumbled blob of facts and feelings – replaces what was flexible functioning. All the sights, sounds, smells, tastes and so on are recorded literally, along with the upset feelings. (The term *distress pattern* will be used interchangeably with *distress recording*.)

Any aspect of a present situation that seems similar to the earlier distressing one can trigger the recording of the old bad experience. We call this 'restimulation'. When this happens, the recording 'falls off the rack' and tends to dominate our feelings and actions. It *plays us*. Instead of responding flexibly to the new situation, we are *pulled to re-enact the earlier distressing experience.* We feel terrible and we do and say things that don't work. We may act out or rehearse the distress recording.

Each time an earlier incident is triggered, our intelligence is once again shut down, this time by recorded distress. The input of information does not stop, however, and this new information also mis-stores. The distress recording gets bigger, has more 'grooves', predisposing us to be upset more often, by more things.

An example of a distress recording

Here is a familiar example. A little boy gets lost in the supermarket, and can't find his mother for five minutes. Both of them become scared. Eventually they find each other. The mother has felt upset, anxious and guilty while the little boy is missing. When he reappears, she feels a rush of relief and anger. She may snatch him up and hug him. He starts crying. She holds him too tightly, saying, 'There, there, you're all right now'. She will probably let him cry only briefly before she becomes impatient. She needs to cry too, but she feels she can't cry in public and may not even know she wants to. Now she is going to be late to fetch his sister from the school. They must go. She holds his hand very firmly, too firmly, so that he wriggles and asks to be carried. She is almost dragging him along. He is still whimpering, but she has no more attention for him. They are going to be late.

> That's enough! Come *on* now! And *never* let go of my hand when we are out shopping! I've told you before! And be quiet, I can't think! We're going to be late for Tracey! No, I can't carry you, I've got all these groceries. You'll have to walk. Be a big boy now.

Maybe she shuts his mouth with a chocolate bar, and he tries to suck comfort out of it as he trails behind her to the bus.

This is hardly child abuse from society's point of view. A harassed mother is doing her best, with no support to draw on. However, for the child his mother's reactions constitute another hurtful experience to add to the first one. During both the initial distress experience, when the child was lost, and the second one, when the mother hurried and scolded him and would not give him attention for his feelings, the little boy's intelligence was temporarily partly suspended. He continued to take in information, but distress in the present stopped him from processing it.

If, when the little boy gets home, he can tell someone about what happened and be listened to, or show his distress to someone who responds in a caring way, this might be a chance to recover from the frightening experience. If no one is able to pay attention, in the future he is likely to feel frightened when he is left with a babysitter and might make a fuss about shopping. He will be 'restimulated' by the similarity to the earlier situation.

There is now a small scar on his flexible intelligence. It acts as a booby-trap, so that his excellent intelligence is no longer dependable. It can be turned off and replaced by rigid, unthinking behaviour whenever anything acts to trigger (restimulate) the old distress. When it is triggered, the whole complex of feelings will come back: 'Mummy left me. I'm all alone. I can't find her. No one loves me. Bad boy. Mustn't cry. Be big boy. Everything is dangerous.' Not only being separated from his mother, but also all the sights and sounds and smells of the shopping street will have become possible triggers of that set of feelings. When triggered, this recording now plays him, and he feels and does things that don't correspond to the present situation and are not adapted to it. Distress recordings do not enhance our survival or the meeting of our basic needs, and they interfere with our enjoyment of life.

Distress recordings accumulate

As we get older, if we are not able to release these feelings, distress recordings accumulate and our tendency to be reminded of them (restimulated) begins to snowball. Every time we get restimulated, feel the old feelings and rehearse the pattern (rigidly repeating some approximation of what originally happened), new elements become attached to the recording. For example, each death adds to the grief for the first one, which was never fully mourned.

We undergo many hurtful experiences that accumulate and predispose us to being hurt again in similar ways. Over time, this accumulation occludes and masks our basically intelligent nature. We are less able to think in an overall sense, and an increasing number of distress recordings have more and more triggers that can set them off. More often, we find ourselves feeling upset, defensive, angry, lonely, confused, discouraged, powerless, inadequate and so on, even when, objectively, things are going well. Because more and more situations are upsetting for us, we tend to limit our lives. We avoid situations that we feel we can't handle, and our lives get smaller.

Another example of a distress recording

Here's another example. Let's imagine that in primary school Eve had to give a book report and was scolded by the teacher and laughed at by her fellow students. Ever after, she is predisposed to be worried and tense if she has to speak before a group. She avoids it as much as possible. However, as an adult,

Eve has to make a report for some business associates. She begins, and then she notices that many of them look bored and uninterested. Because of her earlier hurt, she can't think flexibly and weigh the possible reasons for their behaviour. Their bored expressions have to mean something is wrong with her presentation. It turns out that before she began her talk, this group had to listen to a mandatory, three-hour presentation and were tired and needed a break. Not knowing this, and not being able to even consider such possibilities because her mind has been taken over by a distress recording, Eve can only conclude that they are restless because she is doing a bad job. She becomes more nervous and increasingly stilted in her presentation. Members of the audience shuffle their feet and squirm in their chairs, stare out of the window, and some begin whispering to each other. Then someone walks out, scowling and grumbling. Eve assumes it is in reaction to her terrible presentation, although in fact the man has a headache. Eve becomes panicky, grabs her notes from the podium and rushes from the room.

It's not surprising if Eve is fearful about her next talk. She will do everything she can to avoid such a situation, even if it means not being promoted on her job. If she has to give a presentation, she will be very tense. She will be tense even if the next group is clearly eager to hear what she has to say, and is warm and welcoming. Just standing in front of a group will be enough to trigger the old, bad experience. She will again experience scared feelings and confusion originating in the earlier events – the business presentation, the primary school book report, and (our experience shows) almost certainly one or more earlier events. Perhaps she panics once more, becomes unable to think, and stops in the middle of her presentation. She might feel as if the friendly faces are simply mocking her. Or that her audience is being nice because they feel sorry for her. She will never want to mention the talk with those acquaintances, so she might never find out what they were really thinking – that she was doing fine! This frightening experience adds to the last one. The scar from the previous hurt gets bigger, and more gears are jammed. She is now even more predisposed to get hurt again in a similar way.

Do these ideas and examples fit your own experience? Do you remember a time when you felt as if you couldn't think? What was happening? Do you know someone who always gets upset in a particular kind of situation? Which situations upset you? Can you remember the first time this happened? Can you think of a particular way that you have been hurt over and over again? Have you been aware of being reminded of an old distressing experience by something that happened in the present?

Experience-sharing

Daire: My comment is about the suspension of intelligence. Last summer, my 11-year-old brother and I headed off to climb a mountain, not far south of Dublin. I got lost driving there, and when we finally arrived, it was getting a bit late. I noticed a sign saying the time at which the car park at the bottom was closed up for the night, but we had a few hours, and it's a reasonably straight-forward climb, so we decided to go up anyway. Everything went well, until I managed to get us lost again on the way down. Realising that the car park would be closing soon, I started to panic. This prompted further bad decisions, and we wound up struggling through thorn bushes and crossing strange fields. By the end of it all, we had got directions – barely intelligible – from a man on whose property we wound up, and we found ourselves running along the road trying to get back to the car before it was locked in for the night. My brother was complaining about being tired, and on top of my anxiety about getting to the car, I was feeling ashamed of having failed in my responsibility to organise the climb well. As it happened, a car stopped and gave us a lift to the car park, with five minutes to spare, but I know that the situation up to that point was worsened considerably by my decisions getting worse and worse as I got more and more frightened. It all came back to me last January, when I got lost in a foreign city in the middle of the night. I was bailed out by yet another timely lift (having somehow bumped into another Irish person), but even as we were in the car I was still extremely jittery and anxious, and I now rank getting lost as one of my greater fears.

Katie: I remember a time I could barely think. I had a near-serious auto accident. I was driving along, enjoying the view of the sound and the mountains. Suddenly a car was right in front of me. I put on the brakes, but the road was wet and slippery and my car spun to the side as I braked. I spun all the way around and came to a stop in the other lane, facing the oncoming traffic. Cars careered around me, a couple of them pinging off my car. I remember the stricken faces of these drivers. One car ricocheted off my car's back end with enough impact that the driver had to stop. By this time the oncoming traffic had slowed down, and we were no longer in serious danger. I remember sitting there trying to get my mind to work. It was like I had to operate by the numbers, very slowly, through thick molasses. I said to myself, 'First you need to get out your car registration', so very slowly I opened the glove compartment and shuffled blankly through the maps and the Toyota manual to my car registration. Everything seemed to take a long time. 'Get out of the car.' 'Walk over to the other driver.' 'Give him my insurance information.' 'Get that same information from him.' 'Oh, here come the police.' 'Now, what should I say? Is there anything I shouldn't admit?' And so on, very laboriously.

Caroline: I remember one trigger for the memory of a painful experience. When my father was dying in hospital, the nurses used to bring him cups of tea that would sit by his bedside getting cold because he couldn't drink them. For years after his death, when I saw undrunk cups of tea with a slight skin on, I used to feel the mixture of grief, anger, fear and despair that I felt in those days in the hospital. I've grieved enough now for him and others that this no longer happens.

Emma: I have an example of being reminded of an earlier hurt. I used to hate anyone being late without calling to tell me first. If they were five minutes late, I'd be annoyed and irritated; by ten minutes I was anxious, by fifteen minutes I had them lying dead in a gutter somewhere and felt dreadful. I knew this was all completely irrational, but I couldn't stop the feelings. A few years into using RC, a Co-Counsellor was a little late. I decided to brush my teeth to pass another few minutes and take my attention off the gathering storm of my feelings. While I was brushing my teeth, I suddenly remembered something I had pushed away. About five years earlier, my boyfriend and I arranged to meet one night, but he didn't show up. I waited for him for four hours, spoke to a few people who'd seen him earlier that day, and eventually I went home. I was angry the next day that he hadn't called to apologise and decided to sulk and not call him either. The following day I was notified that he had killed himself the night he was supposed to meet me. I couldn't handle my feelings of anger and grief, and the huge amount of guilt and feeling bad about myself, and no one around me could either, so I had buried them. Whenever someone was late, the feelings from that time were restimulated, but until that morning brushing my teeth, I had no idea why I felt so bad.

Gillian: I have often felt restimulated around my mum. When I was little she was anxious a lot of the time, and she really only talked to me about her fears and concerns. The distress recording that got laid in led me to try and rescue her and make everything all right – I felt responsible for her happiness. After my brother was born – I was nearly 2 – I am told I was quiet, independent and not a bother. When I am with people who remind me of her, I still feel the pull to behave how I did when I was with her.

I loved my brother, he was my mate. He was very musical when he was little and he won a scholarship to a boarding school when he was nine. I was just eleven. It broke my heart when he was sent away. My mum had a 'nervous breakdown' and I started abusing myself because – quite simply – I missed my brother and there was no one to tell (I had learnt to accept blame and not to be a bother).

Since being in Co-Counselling I have done a lot of work on these relationships and reduced the restimulation considerably. I now do much better around my mother. I have many more occasions when I ask for what I want, challenge things, and won't tolerate things that are out of order. My brother and I have a good relationship now, but it's still hard to say goodbye to him.

Neil: For a long time I've had a strong early memory from when I was 5. It is an incredibly vivid memory – almost like a little film. My mum and her sister-in-law have just brought my baby sister home from the hospital. My sister is lying on the sofa in our front room, my mum and aunt have their backs to me and are fussing over her. My aunt is exclaiming, 'Look at her lovely little feet and her little fingers.' I'm standing in a corner of the room staring at their backs, my fists clenched. I am hating the world and everyone in it. It feels like one of those cinema trick shots where you are zooming miles and miles backwards. Over the years I've realised how easy it is for me to fall back into that corner – especially if things are difficult or if people are criticising me. I can get very quiet and sullen, and retreat. It really is like part of my brain isn't working. I'm in deep defensiveness. (It's also scary how much that fits with the typical Northern Irish Protestant response to things.)

Ebony: As a young person, I walked about three miles to school and three miles back, with my oldest sister and cousin. Some other children, mostly older than me, would join us at a particular place. The oldest ones would sometimes (it still feels like daily) run ahead a piece and go around a bend in the road where there was a wooden bridge that spanned some running water. They would yell out a threat to throw us in as they raced ahead. (I am not sure if they threatened this more than once, but I was scared from the first time it happened.) So each day the fear would be restimulated as I approached the bridge, whether the older children were with us or not. Perhaps they were around the bend waiting to throw me into the water! Day after day I approached this bridge with major trepidation. I would be quiet and try to be invisible as I walked across the wooden planks and heard the rushing water below.

Needless to say, I grew up with a fear of bridges and heights, of heights over water particularly. Before I started Co-Counselling I tried a couple of times to fight against the feeling. Once I started to walk across a short footbridge and felt that I could make it. But soon there was an iron grating that one could see through to the ground below. I took two steps onto it and froze. Someone had to come and hold my hand while I backed off. What got restimulated (something I had not thought about) was that the wooden bridge from my childhood had planks that were about an inch apart and one could see the water beneath the spaces. I felt then, like now, that I would fall through the little holes. Totally unreasonable, of course, but distress is not reasonable; it is not intelligent thinking. Because of counselling on this fear, I can now walk across some bridges – if they are not too long and don't have grates or spaces where I can see the water, and if there is a high enough fence or barrier along the walkway.

I have also uncovered an earlier experience. I had an uncle who, when I was an infant and young person, would pick me up and swing me around over his head. So added to this fear of water and heights is a fear of high things in motion. I never learned to ride a bike. I don't like going down escalators as I feel that I will lose my balance; I feel like I cannot get a grip on anything. (Of course, a young one being twirled around in the air by the waist or legs can't get a grip on anything.)

Kerry: As a baby with pneumonia I was left in hospital on my own. Being separated from my family when I was ill, frightened and confused laid in deep feelings of isolation and the distress recording that I was being rejected because I was bad. Over the last few years my partner has been struggling with some early problems of her own and doesn't initiate any touching or holding, and discourages my doing so. I began to feel rejected and bad, and powerless to take any action to change things. Eventually when I began to work on it in sessions, things relaxed a bit. I am hopeful that I will be able to release my feelings from these early hurts enough to think clearly about my current situation.

Rachael: As a parent, because I was treated in these ways as a young person, I sometimes *feel like* if I could hit my children things would be better. I feel like I have to berate them into being timely, picking the dishes up from the table, folding the laundry. I know better, but my hurt recording fills up my brain and makes it seem as if mistreating them will have a good result. These hurts can make it difficult to think about what would really work – in other words, what would be the most enjoyable and efficient way of getting the house cleaned up?

Jenny: I've noticed that people can be compelled by unhealed distresses to do non-survival things over and over again. We may know we are harming ourselves but still be unable to do differently.

Chapter 3

Intermittent and chronic patterns and the inherent human

The question I'm asked over and over is 'How can you tell a chronic pattern?' Well, technically it's not difficult. How do you notice a porcupine's quills? How do you find out if a cactus has spines? You get near them, pay attention, lean against them, notice there's a spine there.

(Jackins 1978c: 160)

Are you being *yourself* right now? Are you *sometimes* yourself? Never? Always? What do you consider to be yourself?

It used to be that when I (Katie) was at a party, I felt ill at ease and self-conscious. Was I being *myself*? There I was, all tied in knots, with a stiff forced smile on my face, unable to be spontaneous, unable to talk about things that really interested me, unable to draw other people out. People didn't seem to warm up to this tense caricature. (Of course, many of *them* were so tied in knots that they weren't really warming up to *anyone*.)

This is what we call an *intermittent distress recording or pattern*. I was not always as tight and inaccessible as I was at a party where I didn't feel comfortable with anyone. With people I was close to, or sometimes even with a warm and welcoming stranger, I could come alive and show lots of what I think is more accurately 'myself'. I could laugh, I could say clever things, I could be warm and outgoing. I *felt*, also, that I was myself – at ease, joyful. And especially, I could think. I could respond to others in ways that worked, that were good for me and for them and for the overall situation. It was so different from the party, where I couldn't seem to squeeze out anything that made anything go well or better – I was just a frozen blob among frozen blobs. I didn't want to be this way, but it was nearly impossible to break out of it at the time.

Intermittent patterns are triggered by particular circumstances and don't 'play' all the time. We get upset under certain circumstances and only under those circumstances. Some people are terrified of injections, of spiders or blood, hate certain foods, or get sad in certain kinds of weather. When the trigger of that particular object or setting is absent, the distress recording does not play. Another example is stage fright. We don't go around 'stage frightened' all the time; we feel that way only when we're on stage or speaking before a group. If we are scared of flying in an aeroplane, we don't usually feel it when we're on the ground. If tests bother us, we don't go about afraid of tests when we're not undergoing one.

We usually consider our intermittent distress recordings to be 'problems' and are able to think about them as separate from ourselves. We also recognise them in others and consider them to be their problems: 'Never say that to your father. He'll hit the roof if you use that word.' Such patterns limit our ability to respond flexibly in particular situations, but we are not continually under their influence, and we haven't identified with them.

Chronic patterns

However, we do come to be identified with some of the distress patterns we carry. When an accumulation of distress reaches a critical point, it begins to dominate our functioning. The rigidities that are part of it become our 'normal' functioning. These rigidities include our beliefs, posture, facial expression, mannerisms and other behaviour. We call these *chronic patterns* – distress recordings that are continually playing unless they are interrupted. 'We "can't remember" that there is any other way to live' (Jackins 1978d: 250). We may succeed in functioning in many different ways, but only within the confines of the pattern. (If we step outside it, we begin to feel the painful feelings and confusion from the incidents that created it.) Chronic distress recordings tend to be regarded and treated as the unalterable 'personality' of the person to whom they are attached. In fact, much of what we call our 'personality' is a composite of distress recordings. We define ourselves, in part, by the *rigidities* that distinguish us from others.

If our friend behaves in a negative and angry way almost all the time, including when there are many good things going on, we can suspect what we call a chronic pattern. His behaviour does fit with something, but it is not the present. His anger was the best response he could come up with in a difficult situation as a young child, and has become part of a distress recording that is now playing him. 'All of our chronic patterns began as brilliant solutions to impossible situations . . . As history, that was a good way of staying alive, because it worked. As a guide to the present and future . . . it's nonsense' (Jackins 1992: 142).

We may notice that our friend's angry ways keep him from making friends. We may be worried about how isolated he is and decide to point it out. However he doesn't brighten up, look at us appreciatively and say, 'Thank you! That's just the advice I've been needing!' Instead, he's likely to respond as if we have given him one more reason to be annoyed and irritable. It will feel to him like we don't understand, like we are criticising him, or any number of other ways based on how he was hurt early on. He's not intentionally trying to thwart us – *his flexible intelligence isn't there to make sense of what we are saying*. There's no point in wasting our time blaming him – he would not have chosen to behave that way if he could think about it at all. If we have an intense reaction to his behaviour, it probably has to do with our own accumulated hurts – for example, having been around people who acted that way when we were little.

If we assume that human beings behave intelligently unless their minds are involved with distress, we may still *feel like* telling him what he's doing wrong, but we know that it probably won't work. We recognise that he had to have been hurt to be chronically angry. Once we have stopped trying to relate to his pattern as if it were him, there are many ways to handle the situation. One thing we can do is to look for a way to reassure him or validate him. If we pay good attention, we can sometimes guess where he might need reassurance. Any thoughtful and precise support we give him will help him to notice reality – for example, that in the present he is not under attack, or surrounded by unhelpful people, or disliked, or undergoing whatever it was that still seems to be happening in the present. But pointing out his pattern, reacting to it, or blaming him for it has little chance of success.

Because his distress has become chronic (he's identified with it) our friend will not be aware that he is playing a record from the past, that he is like a puppet with the strings being pulled by an earlier miserable time. To him, his negative feelings are completely justified by present circumstances, and he will tend to be unawarely looking for their justification in every situation. What someone else sees as an interesting, solvable problem, he might read as an impossible dilemma. What someone else sees as a harassed waitress with too many tables to work, he might see as someone deliberately ignoring him. What someone else sees as a pleasant social occasion, he might judge to be not worth his time because he will be unable to make friendly contacts. He has been hurt in a particular way so many times that this aspect of his perceptions, thinking, feelings and behaviour is no longer flexible. 'The . . . content of a distress pattern is simply the accumulation of superimposed recordings of what went on in a series of miserable once-upon-a-times' (Jackins 1978b: 116).

In the grip of chronic patterns, we are, in effect, living in the past. We may then encounter (baffling to us) upset responses in others, which add to our collection of hurts and add more grooves to our chronic recordings. It's often a mystery to us that our behaviour hasn't worked. We may become defensive and blame others for being upset with us.

Taking the more powerful role in the recording

If a recording of distress has a perpetrator and a victim component, there's a tendency to re-enact the experience of hurt in the more 'comfortable' dominant role. That is, if a child has been beaten, the roles of 'beater' and 'beaten' are both components of the recording. (Recordings are completely literal.) When the recording is triggered, the child will tend to replay it in the 'beater' role rather than the 'beaten' role – although taking the 'beaten' role is also common. In the more powerful role, he or she will 'take it out' on someone, perhaps a younger sibling. Usually the new victim is smaller or in some other way unable to fight back. Often the victim is vulnerable by virtue of having less power in the society. (Harvey offers many illustrations of this tendency to enact a recording in the more powerful role, e.g. his description of how the mistreatment of upper-class children in England prepares them to rule subject peoples. See for instance Jackins 1981a: 165.)

No 'good' distress recordings

No pattern is ever really good for us or for others, although it can sometimes give that appearance. (The rigid, compulsive character of behaviours dependably betrays them as patterns.) Some patterns are welcomed by other people or by society – for example, compulsive responsibility patterns (that someone seems willing to do all the work allows irresponsibility patterns to continue to play out). Some people's patterns may seem charming – perhaps in an early frightening time, charm was the response that seemed to ensure survival – but the person in the grip of such a pattern would benefit from greater flexibility in his or her responses. Some patterns might be socially valued, for example, an accommodating pattern or a care-taking pattern. Patterns resulting from societal pressures can seem to be pro-survival, even though they can 'outlive their usefulness' – for example, a pattern of assimilation to mainstream culture or of suppressing the high spirits of one's children so that they won't become targets.

Chronic patterns that are pervasive in a particular culture are considered to be 'normal' and 'how the world is'. For example, in Western capitalist countries it is 'normal' to want a big house where it is possible to get away from other people (in other words, it is normal to be isolated). Disrespect of young people is a chronic pattern in many cultures, as is disrespect of poor people. Chronic racist patterns are widespread. Chronic feelings of powerlessness affect most people's functioning.

When a person is in a position to have authority over us or can hurt us, we may hate his or her pattern but tend to treat it as something that has to be put up with and worked around. We tiptoe around the tyrannical boss. We swallow our irritation at a bullying police officer. We are forced to tolerate a teacher's boring lectures.

Numbness

Painful feelings can be overlaid by other distress recordings that have a numbing or distracting effect. For example, if small children are given a chocolate bar when they are feeling upset and need attention, it might set up a tendency to crave sweet things whenever they get upset in this particular way. If our lives are particularly harsh, we might become so adept at pushing our feelings down and out of sight that we can hardly feel anything.

Numbness can seem to have survival value in a distressed society. Given cultural prejudice about strong painful feelings, and people's fears about them, we can *seem* to negotiate life more successfully if we don't allow ourselves to feel much. Life may seem to go along more smoothly, but we are missing the chance to recover all of our flexible intelligence and to live the creative lives we deserve. And our wonderful deep, connected, vivid, sensitive feelings are dulled as well as our painful ones.

No blame for our distress recordings

People are regularly blamed for their distress recordings and patterns, whether these are intermittent or chronic. I (Katie) would not be put in jail for being tense at parties (though at the time I did feel as if I was confined in a kind of jail). This hurt recording is unpleasant and undesirable, and perhaps has deeper roots that get in the way of being close to people. But it doesn't otherwise hurt other people. It is fairly benign in its effects. We can compare it to patterns that are not so benign – for example, a pattern that operates as a compulsion to hurt others. A common misperception is that a person who acts such a pattern out is inherently 'evil' or 'bad'. However, even though the behaviour is destructive, the person in the grip of such a pattern is in a situation similar to mine at a party. I used to feel a nearly irresistible compulsion to be frozen, shy and withdrawn, and could barely move against it. This doesn't mean I was helpless, but the force of the pattern was strong. Someone who hurts others is not helpless either, but there is enormous pressure from the recording to act it out.

People have to have been hurt over and over again to be hurtful to others. Some people who have been sufficiently hurt will do extremely destructive things to other people. It can be quite difficult to believe that murderers and child-molesters are fundamentally good. Punishment can seem only too good for them. Even when it is understood that such persons were badly abused as children, the desire to punish remains. A more compassionate approach is well justified once we understand how distress recordings work. The distresses attached to us came from the outside; we did not create them. The hurts that caused them were inflicted on us when we were small and vulnerable and without resources to recover from the hurts. We are *responsible* but we are not *to blame*.

The distinction between the person and the pattern

There is no connection or overlap between our inherent selves and the distress recordings that have become 'attached' to us. Only our inherent selves are *us*. There's no such thing as a 'mean person', a 'stupid person', a 'bad person', an 'antisocial person', a 'despicable person' or any so-labelled person. Such words are tossed around quite casually and yet, when we believe them and act as if they are true, we ourselves are being hurtful. If we treat the child who is hitting other children in our classroom as a 'bad' person, if we use this word or punish that child, we have added to his or her hurt. We have seen the opposite – teachers who can reach for the person behind the hurt, who praise and love a tense, angry child, who listen and who transform that child's life.

We can have some, although usually limited, awareness that the distress recording playing us is not our real self. It's like being the dismayed observer of an out-of-control drama. I (Katie) have 'watched myself' as, in the middle of an upset, I was pushed by feelings and confusion to engage in an angry argument that didn't resolve anything. However, the angry or disrespectful tone of someone's arguments had triggered my earlier times of being disrespected, and the two of us just kept passing anger and disrespect back and forth, with the actual topic of the argument becoming irrelevant. In one part of my mind, I would be saying, 'This is silly and pointless. We've got to stop doing this. It's not going anywhere.' But intense feelings and confusion could make it seem impossible to step out of.

Because we are not the same as our recordings, it follows that there is no such thing as a sexist *person*, or a racist *person* or a classist *person*. Knowing this greatly improves our handling of conflicts in which sexism, racism, classism or other oppressions play a part. Distinguishing clearly between the recording and the person opens up enormous possibilities for cross-culture, cross-race, cross-religion, cross-gender, cross-age connection and caring.

I (Katie) grew up in the Christian religion. My family attended the neighbourhood Methodist church. From an early time I remember the words, 'Love those who hate you. Do good to those who persecute you.' I think this message can be read as, 'Do not treat people as if they are their patterns.' If you love them, often their patterns will be bypassed, the intact human reached, and recovery made possible. Although he didn't put it in these words, I think Jesus realised that it doesn't work to react to rigid unthinking behaviour as if we are dealing with a thinking person. No one is 'at home'. There is no flexible thinking operating to interact with. Such wisdom has been communicated in different ways in other religions and belief systems.

We can love people while still not allowing their patterns to hurt us or hurt others. 'Loving those who hate us' need not be dangerous or destructive to ourselves. Co-Counsellors work at not becoming victims of patterns, even as we love the persons trapped in them. As we release and diminish our own fears and other tensions, we think more clearly and can become skilful at bypassing or interrupting destructive behaviour aimed at us and others. We can prevent destructive patterns from playing out, without crushing, invalidating, punishing or terrorising the persons trapped in them.

The complete distinction between the inherent human being and the attached distress recording is one of the key insights of Re-evaluation Counselling.

Can you connect these ideas with your own experiences? What distress recordings have you noticed in your acquaintances and friends? What has been your reaction to them? Have you tried to 'change' someone? How, and with what results? Is there a negative (or rigidly positive) way that you feel most of the time? Do you remember before you started constantly feeling this way? What in your 'personality' have you been criticised for? How did you react? How might people have been more helpful? Have you noticed patterns that are chronic in the culture you grew up in? Do you remember noticing them and fighting against them as a young person? Do you know people who continually replay the victim role in their behaviour? The perpetrator role?

Experience-sharing

Emma: My mother refuses to be taught anything new. She'd much rather have teeth pulled. She insists she's just stupid, and my efforts to teach her how to play a video or use a push-button phone have been traumatic for us both. I used to think she was just being stubborn. I'd lose patience with her, and then she would get angry with me. This went on for years. A few years ago she suddenly started telling me about the war. She was 8 when war broke out, and she suffered terribly. Her house was flattened, and she was presented with a 'new daddy' and taken all over the country, but she had rarely talked about it. This particular day, in response to a TV programme we watched, she told me about her experiences as an evacuee. She was the only evacuee in her new school. The teacher had her stand at the front of the class and told the other children not to go near her, not to speak with her or play with her, because she was a 'dirty evacuee'. My mum didn't know what that was and felt frightened and humiliated. Her resulting fear of school meant that she couldn't always do her sums or spelling. The teacher would pull her in front of the class and spank her, or lock her in the cupboard for the day, as punishment. She was ritually humiliated and terrorised every day by the teachers and the other children. This went on for two years. After she told me all this, I could clearly see why anything that even vaguely resembles being taught turns my mother into a completely different woman. I also understand why, from my perspective, she was never interested in my education. She went into domestic service at age 14 and never veered from that occupation. She'd already learned as a young child all about cleaning house and serving people, so she felt secure in what she was doing. I still dread her asking me 'show me how to do that', but now I have more understanding of this as chronic distress and try hard to remember.

    Caroline: Probably because I was so isolated as a child, and thought I'd lost my mother for good in the long gaps between feeds, I have a chronic pattern around making and keeping connections. When I meet people, even on a bus or at a conference, and appreciate their qualities, I am reluctant to let them go. I want them to be permanently in my life. They are often flattered and responsive to my friendliness, but ultimately this pattern is impossible to maintain. After a while, I lose some of my first delight in them, and keeping in touch comes to feel like a responsibility. I've found that the most anti-pattern thing I can do is to awarely choose with whom I want to have long-term, meaningful relationship.

Gillian: An intermittent pattern is fear of going to the dentist. This is because I had horrible experiences when younger. As a teenager I actually fainted once at the dentist. I still usually feel scared just before going to the dentist and pretty rigid while sitting in the chair.

One of my chronic patterns has been feeling stupid – a very common feeling for working-class people. With every question I have been asked to answer for this book I have felt, 'I don't know', 'I don't understand', 'I shouldn't be doing this as I don't know enough', 'I am not very helpful', 'Asking for help will just be a bother', 'It's best to keep quiet if I don't know'. I think I was told I was stupid a lot as a child, and, nobody asked me what I thought, what I wanted, or if I had any ideas or wants.

Neil: I first understood the depth of my chronic patterns at a workshop. I'd been to quite a few RC weekend workshops – Friday night to Sunday afternoon – and usually enjoyed them. The first time I went to a five-day workshop was horrific, as I realised that my chronic distress of keeping people at arm's length and pretending I was fine couldn't last for five days in an atmosphere in which people were genuinely trying to behave well and think well about each other. By day four I was very uncomfortable. All my early feelings of not being liked or wanted were running high, and they were so strong I wasn't able to pretend. I remember coming clean at a support group and sobbing at how bad I really felt. I think this was the first time I had noticed how strong the distress recording was and how much it ruled my life. When I came home I had one or two days when the distress was only low background noise, and I found myself smiling at people in the street. On about day two I had my first negative feeling about someone and noticed it with shock.

I have a 9-year-old son, and things go well between us when I see his patterns and distresses for what they are and don't take them personally. He doesn't usually come right out and say what's troubling him – he'll just get cross with me, or his sister or mother; everything we do will be wrong. Just the other week he was being difficult about going to bed – loads of moaning and foot stamping and cries of 'I hate you. You're not being fair.' He just kept repeating he couldn't go to sleep. I could tell I was getting irritated with his 'bad' behaviour, and I felt he was being unfair as I was missing a favourite TV programme. But I hung in with him and kept asking why he couldn't go to sleep and telling him I was sorry he couldn't. Then, out of the blue, he told me about something he'd seen on the news that had really upset him, and he cried hard for about five minutes and then went to sleep with no problem.

Ebony: One of my distresses is about visibility. I used to try to avoid being visible, but now can usually push myself in the direction of reality while feeling the feelings.

I have a feeling of being in danger when I put my voice out to groups of people.

As a young person I got plenty of messages about keeping quiet. 'Children are to be seen and not heard.' We were told to respect adults, and this meant not 'talking back' (not ever questioning what an adult said, so we learned to put no value on what we thought). My religious influences taught me to be 'humble'. Again, not questioning but meekly following. Being black in the US South, my family learned to act 'respectful' and deferential to white people. We were taught to be mannerly to all adults. Historically, as black people, to be as 'invisible' as possible would better assure survival. Being 'uppity' could cause serious harm and even death.

One day I wanted to put my thoughts out on an electronic discussion list. I wrote my thoughts and for several hours edited and reread them and then knew they were as ready as they could be. It took a few more hours to send the email. I felt scared, stupid and worried. What I finally decided to do was to poise my finger over the 'send' button. I took a deep breath and hit 'send' and the email was gone out to the world (as I saw it). I was suddenly visible and scared to death. I immediately closed my eyes, doubled over, grabbed my head in my hands, and said with fervour, 'I'm dead. I'm dead.' And I waited a few seconds for a blow or death. But . . . nothing. I slowly pulled my head up, took my hands down, opened my eyes and relaxed. Nothing had happened to me physically. I now knew that my thinking was out there to be read by the subscribers of the list, and I felt humiliated. The next time I sent an email to a discussion list, I discharged on how humiliated I felt. I literally felt like I could never show my face anywhere and had images of me darting from building to building, walking through alleyways, to avoid being seen ever again.

Early in my Co-Counselling experience I was restimulated by a Co-Counselling teacher's behaviour toward me. I felt she did not like me, and in turn I could not tell I liked her. I decided that any feelings I felt were distress and that I wanted to take charge of what was happening for me. I scheduled a session with her despite in the past not being able to work well with her. I decided that this time I was going to notice the first thing that came up for me at the beginning of the session and stay with that thought or feeling. I did not tell her my plan because I didn't think it would be helpful. I also felt that I could use the session well without much assistance. When my turn came and I started to notice feelings, I took time to notice her, notice that we were together. I felt disappointed, and I said, 'I am noticing a feeling of disappointment.' She asked me, 'Who disappointed you?' My first thought was my sister. This was my sister who had died, and I was surprised at this thought. I had grieved her death, longed for her, missed her, wanted her, but never worked on the feelings of disappointment. I did that day. I noticed that I was upset with my sister for leaving me so early, that we did not get to have a long life together. I cried and cried about my disappointment in her death. From that session on, I did not put my disappointment on this counsellor. I was able to think about her, notice I liked her, and counsel her much better.

Kerry: This is an example of an intermittent pattern: I enjoy dancing to popular music, but I struggle if I try to learn anything with dance steps. Things like waltzes, salsa or Cajun, where you have to count a little and master a simple repetitive step pattern, quickly bring on a cold sweat and I feel hugely humiliated by my inability to acquire this simple skill.

As for a chronic pattern, it's been difficult for me to feel loved. I have concluded I *am*, intellectually (it seems improbable that all these people I love and respect are lying), but I don't *feel* it. I rarely feel clear about what I want. I'm thrown into confusion when people ask me. I am pulled to assist others and find out what they want. Sometimes it seems as if the only way to get some time to do what I want is to be by myself.

Katie: I'm thinking about the difference between the 'pattern' and my inherent self. One of the early rewards of Co-Counselling for me was the sense of direction I could maintain once I understood the difference between my hurt recordings and the person I really am. This meant I was not in any way defined by the load of distresses I was carrying. It meant that I could make good choices even though painful feelings pushed me toward doing things that would not be good for me. I might be in the midst of confusion, but there was a light at the end of the tunnel. The 'bad' feelings I had did not mean I had crossed some line from being normal into being sick – I was intact and fine, with distresses *attached to me*. No inexplicable illness had fallen out of the sky on to me, or bubbled up out of some flaw in my nature. My problem was not a chemical imbalance that needed to be corrected with drugs. My fears were not predicting anything. With even a glimpse of their true character and origin, I could, for example, laugh and shake about these fears in my sessions, with my Co-Counsellor's support. I could begin to break out of rigid behaviour as soon as I had a glimpse that it didn't fit the present situation. I was so grateful to have an explanation for my problems that made sense!

I have gotten rid of some chronic patterns but am also dimly aware that I'm still being affected by others. There are some ways I still rigidly and predictably act and feel *all* the time. It's hard to see these patterns in myself because they are so much a part of the landscape. It's easier to see such patterns in others. But I know that for me, like for everyone, there's a kind of prison cage around me from which I don't ever (as yet) completely break out of. There are ways of acting and being that would be delightful but seem completely foreign. In fact, it rarely crosses my mind that these options exist.

Rachael: When I was a child, there were certain physical characteristics and behaviours that were extremely valued in young people. I felt awful about myself because I didn't look like that or act like that. I spent a lot of time desperately trying starvation diets and reading 'how to' articles in popular magazines like *Seventeen* and *American Girl* in order to 'improve'. After being introduced to Co-Counselling theory, particularly the theory about the oppression of Jews, I realised that those looks and behaviours were highly valued in the majority culture – the Gentile white culture in the United States – and a Jew who could look and act like that would be able to assimilate easily and hide his or her true identity. My behaviour and physical attributes were/are reflective of my Eastern European Jewish ancestry. I could not be mistaken for a member of the majority culture. The anti-Semitism that was forced on my family (and my teachers and some of my friends) drove their relentless criticism of me. For me, the path to self-acceptance and self-appreciation involves discharging all of my own and my people's internalised feelings of self-hatred and self-disgust that the majority culture – and in more recent times, the experience of the Shoah (Holocaust) – forced on us.

Jenny: I have found that arguing with people (with their patterns) doesn't work. I've generally given up arguing, and by having lots of Co-Counselling sessions have managed to stay more loving and be less critical, which has worked better.

Daire: For many years I found it impossible to believe that my friends simply liked me. I would attach all kinds of significance to the slightest look, or intonation, or action, and would question, for days at a time, if this person actually liked me at all. This got to a point where I was becoming quite demanding of my friends, seeking outward and unambiguous manifestations of their true feelings for me, which put quite a strain on many of those relationships. When I began to examine this in my Co-Counselling sessions, I quickly realised that all of my friends actually thought highly of me and felt close to me, and I identified the source of the pattern as an incident on my second birthday. Two girls, of whom I was fond, had given me a homemade badge for my birthday. I broke it, and then convinced myself that they would, consequently, never like me. This was reinforced by the confusion of the people around me: I had suddenly and inexplicably burst into tears, and as nobody knew what was going on, nobody was very supportive, so that I assumed that they didn't like me either. From then on, I unknowingly added more and more people to this list of those whose true affection seemed dubious.

Being able to separate the individual from the distress had enormous implications in the way I viewed everyone around me. At the time I first met the concept, I was being bombarded with the self-righteousness of many of my peers. They preached a policy of 'love the sinner, hate the sin' and made it out to be a trying endeavour. I was suddenly exposed to the simpler, more elegant, and ultimately more practicable idea of 'love the human, understand the distress'. The most obvious consequence of this was in my relationship with my mother.

I had convinced myself that I didn't like her (when in fact it was her patterns I disliked), because it was simply too scary to attempt any other outlook. Once I got through some of my own fear, I was at last able to find some kind of impregnable core to my mother, inside all the patterns, which I could take as representing her. I was then able to build a relationship with this part of her, a part whose existence I hadn't acknowledged before.

Chapter 4

The recovery process

Human beings are equipped inherently, not only with vast intelligence and capacity to enjoy life and other people, not only with the susceptibility to having this endowment damaged and limited, but are also equipped with *damage repair facilities*, healing processes. These processes undo the effects of hurt . . . *whenever they are allowed to work*.

(Jackins 1965: 75 author's italic)

How Re-evaluation Counselling began

Harvey Jackins and his friend Eddie had both been leaders of shipyard workers during the Second World War. They were blacklisted after the war and struggled to make a living. Eddie became a painting contractor in partnership with a younger man called Merle. One day Eddie telephoned Harvey and appealed to him for help with Merle, who had become increasingly irrational to the point where he had driven his family away, had stopped eating and drinking, and would sit alone in an empty room, sometimes screaming. Eddie had taken Merle to psychiatrists, who had said he was a chronic case needing long-term institutional care. Now the neighbours were about to call the police. Eddie asked Harvey if he could help, reminding him that the local hospitals were notorious for electric shock treatment. Reluctantly, Harvey took Merle to his house. He thought he might find a less defeatist psychiatrist, or at least be able to get Merle to eat. He tells the story of what happened in the pamphlet, *How 'Re-evaluation Counseling' Began* (Jackins 1994).

Harvey had no idea what to do with Merle, but he found some books on psychology and kept trying this and that. In response to one of Harvey's questions, Merle began to cry. Harvey tried to stop him but couldn't, and eventually he wondered if Merle *needed* to cry. Harvey would work during the day and sit listening to Merle during the evenings and weekends, and Merle would talk about his early life and cry violently. Eddie's painting crew kept Merle with them in the daytimes, and they noticed a big improvement in him, although he was too weak and shaky to work. After many hours of crying during the evenings and weekends, Merle began to shake and tremble, talking about things that had frightened him.

After a period of shaking, he began laughing. Merle was now back at work and feeling better. He rejoined his family and began to enjoy life again.

This transformation of someone who had been considered incurably ill was so striking that Eddie and Harvey wanted to explore it further. They thought it possible that what had happened was peculiar to Merle, but in case it was of more general significance, they began listening to each other, and eventually to family members and friends. Although no one responded so dramatically as Merle, they noticed enough changes in themselves and others that they continued, and a theory was gradually developed from what they were learning.

Harvey set up a small business – Personal Counselors, Inc. – and tried out his developing theory with anyone who was willing to be a client. With increasing experience and confidence, he gathered a staff around him. The number of clients increased, mostly because those already involved told their friends and acquaintances about their own experiences. Gradually the theory was filled out over many years. An important aspect of its development was that nothing was included in the theory except results personally experienced by those who were practising Co-Counselling.

The discharge process

We have already discussed the good and intelligent inherent nature of human beings, human vulnerability to being hurt, and how the effects of being hurt interfere with thinking in specific ways. Humans also have a built-in recovery process, which we have found to be far more important than has generally been recognised.

Certain physical processes dissolve distress recordings and make usefully available the information previously held in a static form within them. Harvey speculated that these processes were 'used originally in our earlier evolutionary stages for other functions, [and] have been enlisted by us in our development' (Jackins 1997: 23). For example, 'Trembling, the vibration of our muscles, is a means of releasing heat to preserve body temperature. Somehow we attached to it a process for releasing this particular kind of tension which we call fear or terror' (Jackins 1981b: 59).

We have labelled this set of processes and their physical manifestations with the collective title 'discharge'. The tendency to use our discharge processes is 'built in' and spontaneous.

The outward physical manifestations of the discharge processes are the following:

• *Crying*, the shedding of tears, sobbing, and grieving noises if accompanied by tears, associated with the recovery from experiences of loss
• *Trembling or shaking* with perspiration from a cool skin (sometimes but not always accompanied by active kidneys), associated with recovery from frightening or terrifying experiences

- *Laughter*, often with perspiration from a cool skin, associated with recovery from light fear
- *Angry words or sounds, or a 'tantrum'*, accompanied by perspiration from a warm skin and physical movement, associated with recovery from anger and frustration
- *Laughter*, accompanied by a warm skin, associated with recovery from embarrassment
- *Talk* that is non-repetitive, sometimes reluctant, sometimes eager, and often accompanied by relaxed laughter, associated in a more general way with recovery from hurts
- *Yawning* (of any depth or intensity), relaxed stretching and sometimes scratching, associated with recovery from physical tensions and injuries.

Discharge has the dependable and specific effect of draining the tension from a hurtful experience, with the accompanying *re-evaluation* of that experience.

Re-evaluation is the intellectual processing of the information being freed from a distress recording. *Re-evaluation spontaneously follows discharge* as far as the discharge has freed the information to be available. The re-evaluated information can then be used in the same way as information that appears without any distress associated with it.

> Re-evaluation is the word we have chosen . . . to describe the process of thinking through material . . . which has previously been inaccessible because it has been part of a distress recording . . . This re-evaluation process seems to proceed automatically, both above and below awareness, just as far as the previously-inhibiting distress has been discharged.
>
> (Jackins 1997: 23)

Unless discharge has been interfered with in the past or is being interfered with in the present, it will occur spontaneously when we are hurt. We may start discharging while the hurt is still going on, but we will generally discharge more profusely when the hurtful event is over, especially if someone is there who has attention for us.

Any distress pattern can be eliminated completely if discharge is pursued sufficiently. When this is done, the distressing experience no longer has any negative effects. The experience has still happened, of course, but it can now be remembered in detail and no longer has painful feelings attached to it. We are now able to learn from it, and it is no longer able to 'play' us. Many times, after discharging, I (Caroline) have noticed how an event or interaction that had me terribly upset now seems understandable. I can now cope with it rather than feel overwhelmed by it.

Many hurtful experiences (such as a serious car accident) contain several kinds of painful emotion, for example, grief, fear, rage and physical distress. The recovery process tends to progress from the discharge of the heavier emotions to the lighter ones – from the discharge of grief, to the discharge of fear, and then to laughter and anger, and then to yawning and eager talking, followed by relaxed non-repetitive talking. However, because most people have had one or more forms of discharge interfered with and therefore lack easy access to them, people start by discharging in any way they can. (Also, many of us need to take the time to build relationships that feel safe enough for us to show certain feelings and discharge them.)

Fundamentals students often ask if such-and-such isn't also discharge. The answer is that only the above-listed manifestations have been found to lead to re-evaluation – to the processing and understanding of the mis-stored information from hurtful experiences. Many activities are pleasant and useful but are not discharge – for instance, exercise. Some activities tend to *lead* people to discharge, for example, yoga or meditation, but it is the discharge itself that brings the re-evaluation. Some people find that screaming or making certain noises gives them access to discharge, but these are not themselves part of the discharge process.

One of the reasons the discharge process has not been recognised for the important role it plays is the conditioning to believe that if we stop people from discharging – for example, if we stop them from crying or shaking – we have stopped them from *hurting*. We've been made to believe that a person's situation is getting worse if he or she continues to discharge. Despite the folk wisdom, 'You'll feel better after a good cry' and 'Laughter is the best medicine', discharge has been narrowly tolerated (although cultures differ in the value and meaning attributed to the different kinds of discharge). To various degrees, we have all been trained not to discharge.

In Western cultures, children (especially boys) are discouraged from crying and if they do are often ridiculed and shut in rooms by themselves. Children may be criticised or hit if they show anger. We are generally allowed to cry at funerals and for a while after we've lost loved ones, but not to the extent we need to.

When people find themselves shaking, they are likely to look for a way to make it stop. If they are shaking and there is no recent event to attribute it to, they will tend to feel that something is wrong with them. If it keeps up, they might consult a doctor. Yawning is assumed to be a sign of tiredness or boredom and is considered rude. Although laughter is more widely accepted, if we start laughing very hard, we are usually looked at as though we are strange or are called 'hysterical'.

Tantrums seem to be universally frowned upon. However, if a young person can fully vent his or her frustrations – and not be criticised for doing so – he or she is likely to be relaxed and cooperative afterward. If the child does not get the rage and frustration out, we can expect whining, quarrels with siblings and so on.

Human contact and connection, and discharge

Closeness and connection to other human beings is our natural state. Our prenatal development takes place in complete closeness and connection with our mothers. If at birth (assuming no trauma before birth) our eyes are met with loving looks, our bodies are held closely, our minds get a sense of intelligence in those around us, and people are relaxed, warm and welcoming and stay that way, we stay connected and feel connected. We know ourselves to be secure and unconditionally loved. Any break in this loving connection is hurtful (in part, because an infant has not accumulated enough information to make sense of it). As infants we are hurt by loss of connection. We may feel terror because it may seem that we are actually losing our caretakers (as infants this is life-threatening). If the connection is restored and discharge of grief and terror allowed and encouraged, all will be well again. If contact is not restored and discharge not allowed, a distress recording of that experience will result. As we grow up, restimulation generally adds more layers to this hurt. As adults, we try hard to get into close relationships, but even when we do we may still feel alone and disconnected because these distress recordings have not been discharged.

The discharge process is greatly enhanced and accelerated by close human-to-human connection. To seek human contact after being hurt is built into us, just as the discharge process is built into us. This means that both as counsellors and clients we need to overcome (discharge) recordings of disconnection and isolation to work most effectively. Because we get an opportunity to face and discharge these distresses, our chances of having close, caring relationships, including our Co-Counselling relationships, improve throughout our lives. We often learn to be very caring and supportive of our Co-Counsellors.

Do you remember a time when you cried? Shook? Raged? Laughed very hard? Do you remember having any form of discharge interfered with? How often, in what ways, do you discharge now? What forms of discharge were allowed in your family? Which ones were not allowed? How has your ability to discharge been affected by being male or female? Do you cry alone? With other people? Have you cried at certain movies, or while reading poems or stories? Do you find it easy or difficult to talk to someone when you feel bad? Is laughing easy for you? Where have you found closeness and connection?

Experience-sharing

Neil: Before I started using RC I would use music as a way of feeling things – always on my own. Even now there are certain songs that are guaranteed to make me cry, but only on my own. I've tried a few times to use them in sessions but just get self-conscious. I used to watch the last few minutes of the film, *Manhattan*, over and over on video and cry when the actress turned to Woody Allen and said, 'You just have to have a little faith in people', and the film stopped on his face.

My first introduction to RC had been accompanied by loads of crying, so crying didn't bother me when I got involved. I've always found it easier to show my feelings in a group situation than in one-on-one sessions. It feels safer. The whole notion of discharge was a godsend with our children. I really can't imagine how parents cope when they have no understanding of discharge. My second son was stuck in the uterus and was born at home quite dazed and then rushed to hospital. I stayed with him and talked to him in his incubator. I didn't think he understood my words, but I did believe that the sound of my voice would be soothing and welcoming. He would sleep and then wake up and look at me and I would tell him that I was sorry his mum wasn't here and this wasn't how we expected his birth to be. He would have a big cry and then fall asleep. For the first three months of his life he would have a huge crying session with me for about an hour every evening at 7:00. He would scream and be red in the face, and then when he'd stop he'd look at me for several minutes, looking much calmer, and then fall fast asleep. I had a real sense that he was recovering from his birth. I was able to stay relaxed and loving and listen to his screams, and remind him how much he was loved and how sorry we all were that he'd had such a hard start to life. I always feel so sorry for children when they're told to stop feeling things or when parents say things like 'It doesn't hurt that much'.

I think it is hard for men who come into RC and then aren't able to cry much. It always seems that too much importance is put on crying. I also think we get a bit jealous of how easy it is for women to cry. I've had sessions in which I've yawned my head off and felt so relaxed afterward. I've had great sessions in which I've shown almost no emotion but have been able to use my brain and think well about things.

I think being Gay has allowed me more access to my feelings. I think heterosexual men are in a bit of an emotional strait-jacket – a gross generalisation, but with some truth.

One of the most significant things I was ever told was, 'If you've come into RC to feel better, you're making a big mistake, because if you stick at it, at times you will feel terrible'. As I recover from old hurts I'm uncovering things that it upsets me to remember. But I know my life is better. I function better. I think more clearly about myself and situations now than I used to.

I've really enjoyed working on fear. As a Gay man and a Northern Irish Protestant, fear is pretty key to my distress. Making silly noises and letting the laughter bubble up and explode out has been very liberating.

Caroline: My father died when I was 26 and very pregnant. We were living in a house with no bathroom and used to go to the public baths to get clean. I remember shutting myself in this big white-tiled cubicle, turning on the shower to cover the noise, and bawling my eyes out. I felt as if the water from the shower was an extension of my tears, my grief was so great. At the funeral I had not cried at all, as if I would not let other people see how I felt. Now it was such a relief, so healing, to let the tears flow and flow.

When I was 46 I started rock climbing. I was terrified. I used to shake so much that I couldn't climb; my feet would come off the footholds! I would deliberately put my attention on the immediate reality – on the texture of the rock, on the fact that I was currently safe and not falling, on the next move, on my partner's presence. Then afterwards, from the safety of the cliff top, I would shake and shake.

Usually I can't cry when I hurt myself physically. The training to just get up and get on with it was so strong that even though I try to cry (because I know it is healing), I feel bored quickly and the tears dry up. A few years ago I ran into a plate-glass door coming out of the doctor's surgery and really hurt my face. For once, caught by surprise, I started to cry. My face was bleeding, bruised and swollen. A nurse came along to ask me if I was all right and offer me a cup of tea (to stop me from crying). I told her I was fine and just needed a little cry. I cried for a good half-an-hour, despite the fact that this was a relatively public place and several times I had to explain to well-intentioned people that I was fine but needed to cry. My face healed up quickly and completely, more quickly than I had expected.

Emma: Yawning is my main form of discharge. If I can't sleep and I say aloud, 'I decide to go to sleep now', I start yawning and yawning and go to sleep quite easily. I yawn mostly in early evening when I'm physically tired and my body is at its lowest point. Because of my physical impairments my body gets very painful and my muscles get very tense. If, for example, I sit upright at the computer for a few hours, I get muscle cramps and spasms. Since I've been letting myself just yawn and yawn, I rarely take muscle relaxants to get a muscle out of an excruciatingly painful spasm.

Gillian: Before I started Co-Counselling, I would cry, but on my own. I never really got angry. I don't remember shaking. When I started Co-Counselling, the idea of sharing my feelings in front of another person seemed a bit difficult, but what was more scary was the idea that someone would still like being with me while I did that! Early on I noticed myself shaking, for no apparent reason, and able to express angry feelings. Although it felt hard at the time, I noticed I felt more powerful afterward and more confident in myself. I can see now that being female was a lot to do with what sort of discharge felt OK. When I was little, if I showed how I felt, my mum got tense. What I notice now is that if I am crying heavily in a session, it feels as if something is terribly wrong, as if I am not all right. But if I *can* have sessions where I have a good cry, the feeling of walking through fog clears quickly.

Several years ago I led a playgroup along RC lines, which ran for four years. We would let the children discharge in any way they needed to. Often they would cry when a parent was leaving, as they would get to feel what the separation was like for them. We'd just stay with them and let them cry or feel whatever they felt. Sometimes they would distract themselves, sometimes they would want to get on with things, sometimes they would be able to stay with the feelings for a while and have a cry. They would often get upset and discharge when two children wanted the same thing. Of course we'd have to separate them if someone was going to get hurt, but then we would help them work out what they wanted, engage with each other and work out a solution. Sometimes they'd get angry. We wouldn't let them hurt us, but we would let them express their angry feelings, often with us as the target. You can tell how much it helps young children to discharge when you see how bright-eyed and bushy-tailed they are afterwards!

Daire: For a long time, the processes of discharge and recovery seemed to move so slowly that noticeable change seemed impossible – or at least it seemed it would take years to make any headway whatsoever. About a year ago, my ex-girlfriend and I almost got back together. At the last minute, however, she was lured away by another ex of hers. At first I was gutted. So I pulled my father aside, probably barely even said one word to him, but just started crying heavily. I only cried for about half-an-hour or so, but even by that time I was struck by a remarkable change of viewpoint. In place of anger and disappointment, I realised clearly that my ex-girlfriend and I were actually completely unsuited to each other and that she and the other guy were in fact a much better couple. It was the first time I had seen noticeable recovery from distress (re-evaluation) in one sitting. All other areas of my life in which I had made progress had changed so slowly that it was difficult to pin down the change to any particular cause. But after seeing discharge and recovery in action, and happening so efficiently, it certainly convinced me that the process does work.

Ebony: Before RC, I would cry alone at night, feeling sadness, loneliness. In my family we didn't show feelings in public. It felt safe enough to cry a bit publicly at funerals, but it wasn't enough, and I would be choked up with the need to let these feelings out fully. My brother died when I was 12 and he was 7 years old, and I did not feel like I had permission to cry. I closely observed my parents for any sign of tears and grief that would make me feel I could grieve a little. They were mostly not showing grief, so I had a huge amount of sadness that did not get released. Some years later, almost any funeral, even on television, would bring tears – just hearing sad words and watching people grieve. As a social worker I attended two funerals, and even though I did not know the dead person well either time, I sat in the back of the church and wept uncontrollably at the sadness of loss. I remember feeling embarrassed because the families themselves were not expressing much feeling in public. Even though I was not Co-Counselling then, I knew that my crying was not just about this person whose funeral I was attending. I remember what a relief it was to cry like that.

Growing up, I would sometimes be punished by being hit with a switch. Even then, crying was stifled. I would be told, 'Shut up, or I will give you something to cry for.' Laughter was an acceptable kind of discharge, but it couldn't be too loud or boisterous. We were encouraged to be quiet with feelings.

It was a relief to hear that discharge – our natural healing process – was OK to do and OK to show to others. At first it was hard to cry in front of my Co-Counsellors. It felt humiliating to have someone watching me. I'd have the feeling of wanting to cry so badly but holding back. Once in a group the counsellor put her hand between me and the group, and that gave me safety to cry some. I now cry in front of people with much more ease. I still cry quietly and wish I could sob loudly and with abandon – it doesn't feel OK yet to fall apart that much. Also, as a black person, there is the conditioning to be quiet so as not to attract attention. I would love to have a tantrum, but this is also not yet available. When counselling on times of being treated with disrespect – on incidents of racism – what I *really* want to do is run out into a forest, where I can be as loud as I want to, and scream at the top of my lungs.

Rachael: In my first Co-Counselling class the teacher did a lot of counselling of class members in front of the whole group. Every time someone would start to laugh, cry or shake, I would think poorly of him or her. I refused to discharge in any way, having been taught that only weaklings engage in that kind of behaviour. As a Jew, I had learned that having or showing any feelings other than confidence and self-assurance could be dangerous in the majority-culture-dominated society. However, after holding out for six weeks, I found myself running off to the ladies' room, where I dived into a stall, locked the door and burst into tears.

Jenny: In the last five years a lot of old feelings came up for me that made it impossible to sleep unless I cried and shook every day. After getting through enough of the feelings that I could sleep better at night, I have continued to have a Co-Counselling session nearly every day. This now seems like a minimum in terms of what I need to stay in touch with my humanity and function the way I like to. Some people have questioned my having so many sessions, as if it were strange or as if something must be wrong with me. Children, before they are interfered with, cry and laugh and shake and yawn a lot. I don't think it's any different for us as adults. In fact, we need to discharge more because we have accumulated a backlog of distress. When I talk about functioning the way I like to, I mean being able to get close to people, including people from groups I have been conditioned to fear or avoid. I mean maintaining contact with my family and other people who are important to me, being able to keep moving those relationships forward. I mean exercising regularly and not eating in addictive ways. I mean staying on top of housekeeping. I mean working intelligently for social change with a sense of confidence and hope. To seriously attempt to live in this way requires that I get out the bad feelings I have about myself and the frustrations I might attach to other people. I have to discharge, because my old hurts would have me living differently from the way I would like to live. There are also the pressures from a society that is continuously sending out confusing messages about almost everything, including how to treat certain groups of people, how to spend your time and money, how everything is hopeless. I look at all the people who aren't having any Co-Counselling sessions, and many of them are harming themselves with addictions, are at odds with the people closest to them, are spending lots of time and money on 'recreation' to try to escape their bad feelings, are eating and smoking their way to heart disease, are feeling hopeless about the world. I think if they had the opportunity and support to live more outside of their recordings of hurt, they, too, would feel a lot of feelings and would need to discharge a lot.

Katie: In 1986, after about eighteen years of Co-Counselling, an early trauma I experienced came completely out of occlusion. I was engulfed in terrified feelings – in very heavy terror. To make a long story short, I cried, screamed, shook, and was drenched in sweat – while hanging on to my Co-Counsellors – two or three times a day, for two years. Then it was over. Even if I try, I no longer remember what that terror felt like. I got over it. Because the hurt had happened so early, my life had been completely affected by it until I discharged it. After discharging it, I saw everything in a new light, and possibilities opened before me that had always seemed out of reach.

Even though it was very difficult, I kept working half-time while I was going through this. I needed the money, and besides I would have felt even more frightened if, between sessions, I didn't have something to focus my attention on. Also, continuing to be productive was a daily reminder that I was actually fine. I felt terrible, but it was a benign process. Working helped me keep a useful balance between feeling the early feelings and living in present reality.

Another example concerns someone I know who was having what is often called a 'nervous breakdown'. She felt continuously upset, was crying a lot, and felt she could not handle her job or look after her children. She didn't know why she was feeling so terrified and confused. She volunteered that she must be sick. She felt pressure to quickly regain her ability to cope. However, with encouragement from a group of friends, and help with some practical details, she took time off from her job and got some help caring for her children. Some of us stopped by frequently and listened to her talk and cry. This went on for two or three months. It emerged that she was remembering a very traumatic incident twenty years earlier. Up until this time, she had pushed the feelings out of her consciousness, but they were still stored in her mind. She kept apologising for feeling bad, for being so emotional, for having what she sometimes recognised as irrational fears and over-reactions. However, because she was supported and encouraged to carry out the process that was spontaneously occurring, she gradually began to feel less confused and upset. She was able to go back to her job, care for her children, and better understand why she had been feeling so many painful feelings.

Chapter 5

Co-Counselling

You ask your client, seriously, caringly, 'Where are you? Would you really tell me about you?' Then really listen . . . If you are really interested, really paying attention, they will tell you exactly. They will tell you where they are ready to work and what the chronic pattern is doing to them and what kind of assistance they need to go against it.

(Jackins 1978c: 163)

This chapter is about giving and receiving attention and how this exchange of attention has been organised as 'Co-Counselling'. It also describes guidelines for making the practice most effective.

Giving and receiving attention

Needing, seeking, giving and getting attention are all ordinary. They have been human activities ever since we were humans. It's also natural to want to help each other with our upsets and hurts, to turn to others for help, and to give help. Children spontaneously reach for attention, connection and closeness after being hurt unless they've already been discouraged from doing so, and we adult humans – if our hurts do not prevent it – spontaneously and easily give other people the attention, connection, and closeness they need.

We keep trying to get attention

Every day we try to get attention for our feelings. Yesterday, as I (Caroline) drove my colleague home, she listened to me. I was feeling down, tired and annoyed about something going on at work. There was anger and frustration in my voice, but she was able to listen without getting upset herself. I felt better afterward. Later in the journey I listened to her on a similar theme. She isn't a Co-Counsellor. We were just two workmates using a natural process.

On other occasions, people haven't been ready to listen, or simply couldn't, and they've interrupted me right away. Sometimes they have listened but have agreed with all my bad feelings and added some of their own, and we have both ended up feeling worse, or at least with no fresh thinking. Sometimes I have made myself vulnerable and shared something difficult for me to talk about and have been brushed off and felt bruised or humiliated. I haven't reliably found people ready to listen to me about things that have upset me.

Sometimes we might start talking about something that has upset us – for example, a quarrel with our partner – and instead of listening, our friend jumps in and tells us about his experiences with *his* partner. Or he might say, 'Just forget about it. Let's go and have a drink', and the problem is still there waiting for us when we get home. Or he might advise us to confront our partner. So we try it, but because we didn't get to unload our upset feelings first, we can't think well and don't do a thoughtful job of it. Our words and facial expression are tense and angry, and our partner is offended. Then we both say things we don't mean, and add more tension to our struggle with each other.

Cultural confusion about the discharge process has infected our would-be listeners. They themselves were hurt when they tried to use the process, and in their confusion they replay at us what they were told as young people: 'You shouldn't feel that way!' 'You are acting hysterical', 'Get your mind off of it' and so on.

In addition, when we're upset, we often say and do things that don't make sense, and our listeners tend to get caught up in reacting to our illogical statements and actions. Let's say our boss was critical and impatient at us all day. We come home boiling over with resentment. Our partner asks us to take out the garbage. We blow up and, using housework as a pretext, goad our partner into an argument about housework. Our partner thinks we're being unreasonable, and we are. What needs to happen is for everything to stop and for us to get some attention.

The heavy conditioning against showing strong feelings and discharging, as well as having been shut off when we tried to do this, have greatly limited what most of us can discharge and what we can listen to. We aren't supposed to cry much, especially in public. We are allowed to laugh, but not in many situations and not too much. Yawning is supposed to be rude. We certainly aren't supposed to shake or rage – we aren't even supposed to *feel* afraid (especially if we are male) or angry (especially if we are female). Something bad happened to a friend of mine (Caroline's), and she started shaking. She was so frightened by this, she went to her doctor and was prescribed antidepressants in less than five minutes.

Human motivation to use the recovery process is strong. We keep trying in spite of everything. We look for opportunities to have a laugh together. We read books or go to movies that make us cry, or feel fear and tremble. We watch sports and get a chance to shout with joy or frustration or rage about our team's success or the referee's mistakes. Even if someone is only half-listening to us, we often manage to fool ourselves that we really are being listened to, and we use this semi-attention to process our experiences and to free up a bit of our intelligence. Because human attention has not been reliable, many of us have shared our feelings with pets, or nature, or imaginary friends. Many of us have turned to God or some other higher power for caring, attention and discharge.

We are used to managing without much attention. Even as young children we rarely got the sort of attention we needed from the people who loved us. Most forms of discharge have been discouraged or forbidden by society's institutions and values, but luckily talking, and some laughter, are generally allowed. We are able to discharge to some extent in everyday conversations. If that were not possible, we would all be more distressed and rigid than we are.

Experience-sharing

Emma: I learned by age 6 that to be 'good' meant never asking for attention by showing that I was sad or angry or even excited. I so desperately wanted to be 'good', I learned how to feel nothing, apart from a deep sense of shame and humiliation that leaked out from time to time. If I ever showed I was sad, my mum, my Nan, my aunt, my brother and cousins – whoever happened to be around – would sing, 'Em-ma's got the mis-e-ries', or, 'Snivelling in the morning, snivelling in the evening, snivelling in the afternoon.' Often several people sang as a choir. Because my two cousins and I were all subjected to this same humiliation, we turned it on each other at any opportunity. I did get a lot of one-to-one attention from my dad at weekends when my mum was working, and even more from my great-uncle – attention that I enjoyed. I got a lot of attention from my great-granddad, too, though he died when I was 4.

Ebony: A physical injury or sickness would get my mother's attention, and she would care for me to make me better. Physical injuries from accidents worried her, and I ended up listening to her worries and fears. I kept emotional hurts completely to myself. I would cry by myself at times, at the loneliness of it all. I ended up being self-sufficient and attending to my siblings. I would see the younger ones crying and trying to get my mom's attention and would feel envious that they could do that. My high school teachers paid attention to my academic work and gave me praise, and I used that as encouragement to keep going. I think my parents were pleased with me, but they could not say that. They believed one should not praise children or it would give them a 'big head'. Being humble and modest were thought to be good things. I looked for tangible things they did to remind me that they did care.

Neil: There wasn't anyone I could talk to. My parents were too busy struggling to make ends meet. Bringing more problems to them was just not possible. I don't know when I learnt that, but it was certainly early. When I was 8, I discovered US superhero comics, and I escaped into that world. The heroes had 'real' problems, some of which I could identify with, but the biggest thing for me was that no matter how bleak things got or how much it looked as if the villains had won, in the end the heroes would always triumph. I found that important.

Gillian: I don't remember having anyone in particular I could talk to. What I could talk about with my mum and dad was limited (different things with each). If I did discuss anything with them, they always told me what to do. I was never asked what I wanted or how I felt. The person I could turn to was my brother. We could deal with things through play. We played a lot together and could laugh about things and talk a lot. We fought too! But I felt safe with him. It was hard for me when he won a scholarship to a choir school at the age of 9. I was only 11 then. I got lots of pets to compensate for feeling lonely.

Caroline: I don't remember anyone ever paying attention to my feelings when I was very little. As I remember it, I was alone a lot of the time. When I felt miserable, my parents told me I *wasn't* miserable. I could talk to my mother about all sorts of things, and be listened to, as long as there were no bad feelings involved. I used to talk to tiny dolls I had, and later I wrote poems, and wept and shook over them.

Rachael: As a young person I used to lie in bed at night and cry extremely loudly. I would leave the door slightly ajar to be sure that my parents could hear my wails. My father would come upstairs, sit on my bed and give me a lecture about being self-indulgent and thoughtless of other people's feelings. However, I persisted in my attempt to get attention for my lonely feelings.

Kerry: One of my most significant early connections was with my dog. He gave me lots of attention when we were playing together. There was something about the unconditional welcome, the delight he had in me, that relaxed me. I knew I wasn't going to mess up this relationship. I could get physically close to him without feeling threatened. Later my sister could pay me some attention too.

Co-Counselling

In the 1950s, about the same time Harvey Jackins and his associates glimpsed the importance of discharge, they experimented with *taking turns* as counsellor and client. The results were encouraging. It turned out that people can very usefully *exchange* attention with each other – especially when both people have agreed to encourage our built-in recovery process. This was an important discovery. It means that it is possible for ordinary people to assist each other to recover, including from the most severe and prolonged hurtful experiences. The Re-evaluation Counselling project has gathered a large amount of experience and data about making the exchange of attention work well. We've learned much about the client and counsellor roles and how to function well in each of them.

Basic agreements

Co-Counselling works best when participants follow some guidelines. We talk about these guidelines early on and ask people to agree to follow them.

No socialising

If we meet someone in a Co-Counselling class or other Co-Counselling activity, we are asked to restrict our relationship to Co-Counselling (Jackins 1985: 197). We don't become business partners or lovers, or go on a trip to the beach together, or borrow tools from each other, or recommend a good dentist. This is the 'no-socialising policy'. It does not apply when people have formed a relationship before becoming Co-Counsellors – we can add Co-Counselling to existing relationships and it does not seem to create the same kinds of difficulties, although even then it is important to be clear about which role we are in at any given moment.

Co-Counselling relationships are real. They are close and deep, but not wide. Their well-defined purpose gives them power. There are few distractions from the task at hand: to exchange attention and think as clearly as possible about another person.

Co-Counsellors sometimes do things together that *look like* socialising – go to each other's houses, ring each other up – but always with the purpose of helping each other emerge from distress. They might visit each other in hospital or even go shopping or rock-climbing together, but their joint activity would be for the specific purpose of discharging painful emotion associated with that activity, or breaking through some limitation. At Co-Counselling workshops, people eat together, and play volleyball or go for a walk together in the breaks, while keeping in mind the basic purpose of helping each other get free from distress.

I (Caroline) am thinking of a man who was in a Fundamentals class I once led, and who was very lonely. He discharged in class and had Co-Counselling sessions about his loneliness and his longing for female company. The no-socialising policy made it possible for women in the class to listen to him lovingly without feeling pressure to go to his house and try to 'make everything all right'.

Confidentiality

We are asked to respect confidentiality. Anything a client says in a Co-Counselling session or group is not to be repeated to anyone. It's not to be talked about with Co-Counsellors (even if they were there at the time and heard what was said) or anyone else. It must not even be repeated to the client himself or herself outside of a session. This strict understanding of confidentiality helps me (Caroline) feel much safer. I am freer to be open without worrying that what I work on will be passed on or gossiped about, or come back to haunt me in some way. I also like the fact that what I say won't be brought up in conversation later. It means that I can play with ideas and feelings without having to be consistent. If I dip into some difficult or painful feelings, I can choose for myself whether to do so again, and when to do it.

No mind-altering drugs

We have a policy about mind-altering drugs. We meet for the purpose of discharging hurts, and it is counterproductive to use substances that numb us and interfere with the process. All mind-altering drugs, including alcohol, tobacco, street drugs and psychiatric drugs, tend to inhibit discharge and re-evaluation. They also *install* recordings that later have to be discharged. Fundamentals students are encouraged to give up all of these substances, or as a first step, not to take them before coming to class or to their Co-Counselling session. When someone decides to quit any of these substances permanently, good support can be organised – for example, a Co-Counselling session every day or some one-way attention.

Equal time

Usually by the second meeting of a Fundamentals class, participants have chosen someone to Co-Counsel with outside of class. The pair will meet weekly, exchanging equal time being listened to, maybe beginning with half-an-hour and working up to one hour each.

One person takes a turn as counsellor, and then the roles are switched and the former counsellor becomes the client. Each person gets equal time being listened to because it's understood that everyone has been hurt and everyone needs attention. Our hurts can be very different – one of the pair might feel desperate and needy and the other calm and in control of his or her life. However, our assumption that we have all been hurt, we all need attention, and we are all equally entitled to it, is important. It doesn't make sense for one person to get all the attention. We avoid getting stuck in always being the attention-seeker, or on the other hand, the ever-patient listener. An equal exchange is fair.

We are peers

Co-Counselling is set up to be a relationship between *peers*. Functioning as peers is consistent with the assumptions we have made about human beings. We are all very intelligent. We are all vulnerable to being hurt and having our intelligence interfered with. We have all, without exception, been affected by past hurts from which we need to recover.

Even if one of the Co-Counsellors is experienced and the other a beginner, the two Co-Counsellors function as equal partners. Neither one is held up as the 'expert'. Neither one can claim any basis for dictating to or advising the other. To be in the counsellor role in a Co-Counselling session does not require an academic degree or what we usually think of as expertise. As new Co-Counsellors, we often counsel experienced ones well, because listening with respect and interest and being our human selves is so central to being a successful counsellor.

Assisting the client to discharge

In Re-evaluation Counselling, the counsellor's caring, the quality of the attention and the increasing safety of the relationship, are his or her most basic and important contributions to the session. The attention (as well as any interventions) are for a *specific* purpose. It's quite a different role from the role many people associate with the word 'counsellor'. In Re-evaluation Counselling, nearly *everything* the counsellor does is aimed at assisting the client to 'cross the bridge' to discharge – to the crying, shaking, perspiring with cold and warm sweat, raging, laughing, interested non-repetitive talking and yawning, that release tension from recent upsets and stored-up hurts and give back to the client his or her clear thinking. In no way does the counsellor do the thinking *for* the client. Once freed by the discharge process, the client's own thinking is sufficient. In fact, it is the only thinking that will precisely handle his or her completely unique circumstances.

Because we practise *Co*-Counselling, because both people have turns discharging, we have increasing 'slack' each time we are in the role of counsellor. The slack (awareness, free attention) that we gain from discharging is a key factor in being an effective counsellor. A client's ability to discharge is greatly affected by how much we, as counsellors, are really present. If we are not ourselves receiving effective counselling regularly, our ability to elicit and assist discharge from clients will stay limited or even regress as restimulation adds to our own tensions.

People are usually surprised at this new way of being a helper. There is no advice-giving, no interpreting, no need to figure out the issue and offer a solution. As Re-evaluation Co-Counsellors, both client and counsellor come to the session with the specific intent of unravelling stored distresses. Some clients have relatively free access to the recovery process. It may take only a warm, caring listener for them to break into tears, or trembling, or laughter. For other people, it can take time to regain full access to the discharge process.

Each person has a completely unique collection of experiences, including experiences of how their caretakers reacted when they talked, cried, were afraid, were angry or laughed. For example, if our parents were relaxed and welcoming when we confided in them, we may find it easy to verbalise what we are feeling. However, these same parents may have become upset if we were angry, and, as a result, angry feelings are now less accessible to us. In general, men find it more difficult cry, and women find it more difficult to feel and express anger. The counsellor needs to welcome whatever discharge is available to the client.

Contact with reality and contradicting distress

Distress recordings cause rigid, usually negative perceptions and feelings that can seem completely believable to the client. When old hurts are throbbing, or when they operate chronically, the client will feel convinced that 'Nothing will ever work out for me', or, 'I shouldn't *have* to keep my temper', or, 'Nobody likes me', or 'It's impossible to communicate with *him*', or 'I can't stand *that* group of people', or, 'I'm just fine, just fine, just fine', or any of a million other recorded messages.

For discharge to take place, particularly the discharge of chronic distresses, it's perhaps essential that the client notice the safety and goodness of reality – the reality of the counsellor's caring, the reality of unlimited possibilities and options. We can see this principle in operation when we cry at the happy ending of a movie. The hero has gone through terrible experiences but finally triumphs in the end. The victory gives us a glimpse outside of the distresses that the hero has endured and, identifying with the hero's struggle and triumph, we can let go of some tension from our own struggles. We cry and begin to recover from some of our hurts.

It's fairly easy for an onlooker to notice when someone is not in contact with reality. We've all had this experience. For example, I (Katie) have a friend who feels bad about how she looks, yet I and others can see that she is attractive. I know someone who disparages her accomplishments, yet her many achievements are obvious to me. We know people who feel unhappy no matter what is going on, and it may be quite clear that these feelings are not about the present (they are recorded feelings from unhappy times). The counsellor notices such rigidities in his or her client and does things – and encourages the client to do things – that show these rigidities for what they are and in that way make them available for discharge. The counsellor, easily seeing a more positive picture, often encourages the client to take a stand against the distress.

The client's hurts have skewed his or her perspective. Part of the counsellor's job is to notice this distortion of perspective and to be, or offer, a truer view, and to do this in a way the client can notice. We call this a 'contradiction'. We use the word 'contradiction' to name any factor in the session that allows the client to see that her or his distress recording does not represent present-time reality. Contradictions interrupt distress recordings. When the contradiction is accurate and sufficient, the client will always discharge.

To contradict the distress enough for it to discharge, a client often needs to do more than say words. Tone of voice, posture and facial expression can be changed to better represent the client's true self. It's fine to be loud, or to move, or to use force. For example, someone who always feels small and powerless can loom over the counsellor and in a booming voice tell the counsellor everything that's going to be different from now on, or the person can push against something and loudly argue with the false messages she or he got from parents and teachers. In Co-Counselling, both the client and the counsellor look for contradictions to the client's distress.

To eliminate our chronic distress recordings, we need to act outside of them in our lives. For example, we can't keep acting like a grouch and have that pattern discharge efficiently. We have to struggle against our patterned behaviour to be able to efficiently discharge the hurts that became these recordings.

We need close, loving relationships to be able to discharge easily, especially on our heavier hurts and chronic distress recordings. Much of our job as client is to discharge the distresses that would make us not trust people, that would make us feel unworthy of people and be separate and isolated from them – including from our Co-Counsellors.

We take a big step simply by turning up at a Co-Counselling session. Most of us have to step out of isolation, numbness, fear and mistrust just to do this. Many of us contradict patterns just by trying to talk about ourselves. Most of us have been trained to be secretive about our struggles, afraid something bad will happen if we tell the truth about what goes on in our minds. We find that our Co-Counsellor's respect for us is not diminished when we reveal our doubts and hurts. We listen to others and realise that we are not the only one who, for example, wakes up in the morning feeling dread or self-reproach, or with lists of things that ought to be done. Sharing our struggles contradicts a common self-perception of being uniquely bad, weird or otherwise different.

We also make our lives better just by going to our Co-Counselling session because, whatever else happens, we get to be close to another mind in a way that doesn't happen much in other contexts.

Confidence as counsellor

The most important contradiction to the client's distresses is the counsellor herself or himself. This is hard for beginning counsellors to grasp. They are often eager to be taught techniques, or special methods, or tricks. This is partly because we have been made to doubt that as human beings we are 'enough'.

Counsellors can help clients notice that they, the clients, are in the presence of another human being who cares about them, who is thinking about them, who wants to be close to them, who is interested and paying attention. Counsellors can assist clients to notice this in all sorts of ways – with words, touch, facial expression and eye contact. The client may not want to look at the counsellor, but if the client does, he or she needs to find the counsellor's eyes looking back awarely and the counsellor's face expressing unworried liking, interest and respect. (We need not pretend anything as counsellors. As we reach for our genuine love and respect for the client, our facial expression will follow suit.)

A collection of hurtful experiences – including society-wide misinformation about human nature, and not being respected when we were young people – have caused most of us to feel inadequate as counsellors. However, we *are* enough. To be our human selves is enough. When we were babies and young people, if our parents even approximated thoughtful attention and caring, we spontaneously began to discharge our hurts.

Part of the process of learning to be a counsellor is peeling off all that has left us feeling less than a full human being with important resource to offer. Most of us have to discharge and re-evaluate many layers of self-doubt in the process of becoming a confident resource for other people. Because we ourselves are systematically discharging, we get better at expressing caring and love, and our mind becomes sharper at finding contradictions to our clients' distresses.

A useful analogy

Harvey Jackins (1983a) compared the counsellor to a bagpiper. The bagpipes – an ancient wind instrument – have a drone pipe that plays a consistent background note, while the chanter plays the melody. If the counsellor's basic attitudes toward the client are of approval, caring, respect and confidence (the drone pipe), the client will have a good session even if the counsellor is not yet sure how to play creative melodies on the chanter (directions, encouragements, *specific* contradictions to the client's particular distress).

Each of the attitudes mentioned – approval, caring, respect, confidence – is crucial. It's difficult to open up to someone who does not approve of us. Or who can't show they care about us. Or who doesn't respect us. Or who has no confidence in us.

To get in touch with these basic attitudes, we can take a moment at the beginning of a session to remember that we are good and enough, that our presence can make a big difference to someone. We can take time to remember that our client is also a good, competent, intelligent person. We can review in our mind all the evidence of his or her true nature and capabilities.

Co-Counselling goes better if the counsellor assumes that the client is always doing his or her best. Harvey wrote:

> Sometimes a counselor complains to me 'This client doesn't respond well. He has barbed wire wound tightly round his wrists, the despicable creature.' But that is *exactly* what he is asking for help with! If his request for help comes out in offensive language, that's the way the distress is in there.
>
> (Jackins 1978c: 172)

Gaining access to discharge

When we were very young, if we had been hurt – for example, stuck with a nappy pin – we would begin to cry. If a parent removed the pin and stayed with us, relaxed and warm, we would cry harder. It's likely we would cry for quite some time. We would use the opportunity to cry out additional hurts we had been saving for such undivided attention. I (Katie) am still able to be this direct about some types of upsets. For example, when I came close to a bad car accident, I told the story to anyone who could pay any attention at all, and shook and laughed as I told about it.

However, the path to discharge can be less straightforward. When a hurt includes feelings of vulnerability or confusion, we need a listener whose distresses are not triggered by this, who can continue paying relaxed thoughtful attention to us. When we feel bad about ourselves, we need someone who is not confused about our goodness, who is confident that we are fine. Often, when we are upset, we blurt out things that don't make sense in terms of the present situation, and we need someone with us who understands that. In general, we need someone who will encourage us to release our emotions, or at least not stop us from doing so. Given social conditioning, most of our would-be counsellors are unlikely to play this role very well.

To add to the difficulty, by the time we're adults we have accumulated many undischarged distressful interactions with people, particularly from times we tried to get attention for our hurts. Our recorded messages will tell us that it's not safe to rely on people when we're hurting (or, for many of us, at all).

As typical adults, we've had to cope for a long time without being able to discharge much. A lot of hurt has accumulated, and it's as if our hurts are a tangled brush pile. Some of the biggest hurts are down at the bottom. We can't be aware of them enough to discharge them until the twigs and branches on top of them have been removed.

By the time we are adults, most of us have forgotten the big early hurts. They have become buried and numb. We have a fuzzy awareness that life is not all it should be, that we don't feel happy a lot of the time, that many situations are confusing and difficult, but we don't connect this to events earlier in our lives. This is the situation most of us find ourselves in when we begin a Fundamentals of Co-Counselling class. It often takes a few classes to even realise we have been hurt.

What this means is that strategies are useful in finding hurts and beginning to unravel them. The following are some general ones. Using these strategies in sessions will increase our access to discharge, and our lives will go better as well. Using these strategies in our lives will make the discharge process works increasingly well.

Attention on reality

We humans are good. We mean well and want to do the right thing. We live in a world of great wonder and beauty – of music, poetry, art, knowledge, of infinite opportunities for learning, countless people to love and be loved by, exciting adventures, worthwhile projects – all around us, always. We can enjoy these good things as a way to live fully. We can also use them in sessions to contradict recordings that pull our attention so far into the old hurt that we believe the recordings, act them out continuously and can't discharge them. For example, we might read a beautiful poem in session, one that moves us to tears, or look at a photo of someone we love.

Feeling our feelings

As a point of clarification, *feeling our feelings* is not the same as believing or acting out the distressed ones. Of course some of our feelings are appropriate to the present. We may feel joy at the sight of spring leaves or when we are reunited with someone we love. We may feel grief at a recent loss, or anger about injustice that's happening right now. Strong feelings are part of being alive and aware of what's going on around us.

It is also a good thing when we can feel the painful emotion from past hurts. Most of us have tried to numb these feelings in some way or push them back down. We have been afraid of getting stuck in them because we have been prevented from discharging them. Most of us have had to deny our heaviest painful feelings and our deepest hurts because this seemed the only way we could survive. We've been made afraid of strong emotions. However, they aren't dangerous.

It can be particularly difficult for us when painful feelings seem to be overwhelming (a reason many people seek counselling). In general, people are unable to give us the relaxed, confident attention that we need. They may communicate that something terrible is happening to us, or give us unhelpful advice, most of it including the urgent message to *stop feeling and get on with our lives* (however unsatisfying those lives may have become). We may be so shamed and criticised for the condition we are in that we make huge attempts to push all the feelings back down again.

Our distressed feelings don't represent the truth about ourselves or the world but are a benign aspect of ourselves. When we feel grief, terror or embarrassment, these feelings are our allies – they are letting us know we need to recover from something. Especially when we have someone's aware attention, feeling our feelings is a first step to discharging them. Therefore, we do need to feel. Sometimes we need to feel very bad in the process of discharging our hurts. Sometimes we need to feel bad for quite a while to reclaim the greatness of our lives. We will need to feel grief and fear as we discharge our chronic distresses. We will be well rewarded for doing so.

Contact and closeness

It is within our close relationships that we find love, caring, sharing and much of what we consider a good life. It is also in relationship to others that we find sufficient contradiction to our distresses to discharge them well. For example, a close and supportive relationship will contradict the loneliness or harshness of earlier times and make these hurts accessible for discharge.

Because we have been hurt, we commonly seek relationships both for the inherent joy and interest of being with another human, and (usually unawarely) for enough contradiction to our distresses to discharge them. (People will often hold on to a difficult relationship if it meets one or both of these needs even a little.)

It is also common to use relationships to try to fill old recorded ('frozen') needs. These recorded needs have us *compulsively* seeking good parenting, closeness, excitement, love, praise, undivided attention or whatever else we may have missed early in our lives. For this reason, close relationships tend to be a turbulent arena of life. We need connection and closeness and cannot live well without good relationships. At the same time, because we have been hurt, we often have irrational expectations of people we are close to.

Because of pressures from unreasonable expectations and other distresses, the Co-Counselling relationship has been structured carefully. It is set up to maximise caring, safety, good attention and other contradictions to distresses, and to minimise opportunities for restimulation and attempts to meet 'frozen' needs. The no-socialising policy counters the tendency to act on frozen needs (you are not to meet for purposes other than exchanging attention and discharging), and instead encourages Co-Counsellors to *discharge* hurts from not having important needs met early in life. (With enough discharge, the rigid, compulsive character of these needs – their 'frozenness' – is eliminated.) Co-Counselling relationships become important, safe and close as a result. People use their freed-up thinking to solve problems in their non-RC relationships, to have more relationships, and to make these relationships more and more satisfying.

Aware physical closeness generally increases safety and contradicts distress. Harvey Jackins wrote that he was slow to realise how important closeness is.

> There was no closeness for anyone where I grew up. It took my clients in the throes of heavy discharge to convince me that I should hold their hands, or, later, put my arms around them. I suffered terribly from my own fear and embarrassment, but I did notice what a big difference it made in their ability to discharge.
>
> (Jackins 1978b: 120)

Co-Counsellors often hold hands. Sometimes a warm embrace allows us to actually notice that we are not alone, that we are with a caring human being. We can often feel fear more easily or cry more deeply in the security of an embrace. The counsellor needs to gauge the effect of any closeness that is offered. If it leads to safety and more discharge, it makes sense. If the client shrinks back fearfully or stops discharging, the counsellor should return to an earlier amount of or no physical contact. Closeness is scary for many of us because we were hurt while we were physically close to non-thinking persons. (Some others of us like physical closeness but discharge more if there is a little distance, perhaps because as young ones cuddling was used to soothe and silence us.)

Oppression has struck a particularly heavy blow in the area of close human relationships. The mistrust and fears engendered by systematic mistreatment have separated humans from each other – young from old, male from female, black from white, Muslim from Jew and so on. As we discharge the hurts from oppression, it's easier to make close connections across former barriers. (See Chapter 6 for more discussion of oppression.)

Appreciation

The nature of our hurts, and the negativity and put-downs common in our societies, leave most of us feeling less than good about ourselves. We can often discharge immediately if someone says good things about us. Our recordings also say false, negative things about other people, and if we praise and appreciate others, we will often cry, laugh or shake along with them.

Most of us have been so rarely appreciated and validated that the times we have been stand out like beacons. Before I began Co-Counselling, I (Katie) remember only two or three times when someone's appreciation of me reached me deeply. I would often refer back to those times when I was feeling bad and needed something to hold on to. In our lives, we make a huge difference to people when we appreciate and validate them. In sessions, it can release discharge when as counsellors we express appreciation for our clients – for their courage, their successful struggle, their human qualities. A Co-Counsellor who knows the client well can tell what specific acknowledgement and appreciation will go to the heart of the client's distress and melt it into discharge.

Most of us need validation and acknowledgement – a lot of it. We try to be good to others. Many of us pour our hearts out again and again, but because people are preoccupied they usually don't let us know that they notice. It can seem like we are trying hard and doing our best in a total vacuum. Our days go much better when people tell us they have noticed us, our efforts, the results of our efforts – and that it matters to them. Our sessions go better when our counsellors can do this.

Feel feelings; act on thinking

When our feelings push us in directions that don't make sense, we can act logically in accordance with what we know is good for us and for others. We are patient with our children even though we've had a bad day and feel like snarling at everyone. We study for a test because it's a gateway to something we want, even though right now we'd rather be going to the beach. We don't eat the third piece of cake in spite of our 'sweet tooth'. We go to our Co-Counselling session even though it would be more comfortable to stay numb. This principle is especially helpful as we confront the addictive pull of chronic distresses. The recordings pull us to re-enact them rather than respond in new ways in present time. Every time we resist the recordings, we increase our access to discharge and recovery.

Taking charge, taking leadership

We can refuse to occupy a victim role. We can take initiative in any situation and make it better – we don't have to wait for another person to take charge. We contradict feelings of powerlessness when we take initiative. Working on hurts from oppression often reveals the extent to which we have unawarely acted as victims. It can be uncomfortable, but freeing, to realise that we are no longer victims – we just *feel like* we are – and that we can always take charge, even in interactions with those by whom we felt intimidated or dominated.

Many Co-Counsellors have found that taking a leadership position – for example, teaching an RC class – is a great way to act in accord with our true power and to feel and discharge fear. In our lives outside of RC, taking action with others to change something that is unjust or wrong can help us get free from early recordings of submission, isolation and hopelessness.

Holding 'directions'

We need to take our everyday lives out of the grip of irrational attitudes and behaviour and unnecessary limitations, even as we discharge in our Co-Counselling sessions. 'Directions' are ways of contradicting a pattern by persistently holding to a course of action or a perspective that goes in a different direction – away from the distress.

As we become aware of misfunctioning, of the patterns that were forced on us by our hurts, we move against them. We make 'practice' or real decisions in sessions, we act on them in the world, and then we bring the feelings that come up back to sessions. For example, if fear of failure or of not being clever enough has kept us from learning the new things we want to learn, we might go back into education. We push ourselves to think and act positively if we have been caught in a negative or hopeless pattern. We try to make friends if we have been shy and withdrawn. We stop frenetic activity if that is how we have kept our feelings at bay. We reach out to and make friends with people of different ages, ethnicities, genders, social and economic classes – not only to greatly enrich our lives, but also as a way to exit from distress-made boxes.

Telling life stories

Telling life stories is one good way to approach being a client in a session. Tell your life story any way it wants to come out. At first, people often tell it in ten minutes and think that's all there is to it. For example, here's how I (Katie) might have told my life story before I began Co-Counselling:

> I was born in Seattle, Washington, USA. I have four siblings. My older brother is nine months older than I am, and we were and are close. I got good grades in school. My family liked the out-of-doors, and we camped and skied and hiked. I went to college in Pennsylvania and dropped out in my senior year and got married. I got divorced four years later. I've had several different jobs. I've had a few close relationships. I feel depressed and anxious most of the time. I guess that's about it.

This would have been my life story (probably with a few more details) before I began Co-Counselling. Now when I tell my life story I can fill it in with hundreds of details. I know where the painful feelings are in my story. I have also recovered many memories – for example, of the house I grew up in, my third grade teacher and so on. As we tell our life stories again and again, we recall memories of forgotten people, times and places – precious memories, both pleasant and painful, that our lives have been built of. We discover forgotten painful emotion. We also get an overall perspective on our lives. We contradict the numbing effects of distress that would have us believe that our lives have been uninteresting or unimportant. We can tell the same story to different people, and each telling will be a different experience. It has often made me (Caroline) discharge to notice my counsellor's perspective on my life, which tends to be far more compassionate and appreciative than my own.

These are some of the most basic ways of approaching our distresses, both in sessions and outside them. Many more have been tried and described. We refer you to *The List* and other books by Harvey Jackins. Also, *Present Time*, our quarterly journal, is a collection of experiences using the Co-Counselling relationship and the discharge process, as are the many journals written by and for particular constituencies.

Experience-sharing

Neil: One of the things I enjoy about being a counsellor is that it gives me the space to see someone as a human being. Sometimes I've counselled people whom I'd previously felt I couldn't stand because there was something about their distress that restimulated me. When I've been their counsellor, I've seen their struggle and often I've been able to feel genuine affection and counsel them well.

Gillian: I like the way Co-Counselling works for all kinds and ages of people. Most of us in this contributors' group are in our forties or older, but it works just as well for young people, and I'm committed to making sure they get a chance to use it. Recently I was a support person at a workshop for young people. With some other adults, I helped cook for the workshop and spent time with some of the young people. Their workshops are set up a bit differently from adults' workshops, and they need some support from adults so that everything goes well. At this workshop, there were about twenty young Co-Counsellors, ranging in ages from 10 to 21, led by a young person, and they ran the workshop. The adults were there to support the leaders, giving them attention if they wanted it, to help prepare the food, and in general to act as allies for the young people.

Katie: I remember my first Co-Counselling class and being expected to choose and have sessions with a Co-Counsellor. I had joined the class because I had been feeling anxious and depressed for a long time, had separated from my husband, was overwhelmed as an elementary school teacher and about to quit, had lost my confidence, and was discouraged about my future. At the time I didn't see myself as someone who could be of much help to anyone else. Nevertheless, I was expected to hold up my end of a Co-Counselling relationship with someone in the class, and this gave me increasing confidence that I could be helpful to others. I began to get over the feeling that something was uniquely 'wrong' with me. I soon found out that my Co-Counsellor didn't 'have it together' either, although I couldn't have seen that just by looking at her. The picture began to fill in that everyone has big struggles. I didn't see that picture in my usual life because everyone was so busy coping and trying to look OK. Because I was both client and counsellor, it was less likely that I would attach unreasonable expectations to my counsellors or expect them to never have any troubles of their own that I would have to be sensitive to.

Another benefit of Co-Counselling has been access to the thoughts and feelings of a wide variety of people, people from many different backgrounds. I'm white, female, Protestant, heterosexual, middle class, a USer, and now, an elder. I've had Co-Counselling sessions with African Americans, men, Catholics, Jews, Arabs, Gay men, Lesbians, working-class people, owning-class people, people from many different countries, young people and others. I've learned so much.

Caroline: One of my most important Co-Counselling relationships is with someone I don't see often because he lives a long way away. I'll call him B. B manages to communicate to me that he knows, as a matter of course, how good I am. He is completely unworried about my ability to come through whatever I happen to be struggling with. He is concerned when bad things are happening in my life, but there's a way he knows and communicates that I am and will be all right. I think if I were to die he would have the same attitude – that sounds odd, but I find the thought comforting and relaxing. When I am with him, it feels as if I can put my anxieties down at last and rest. I reach for that with others, and having achieved it with B does help me get there more often in other relationships.

I first began to get close to B when he counselled me so well that I felt a rush of gratitude. Although he had counselled me well, he seemed not to expect others to be there for him. I decided that I would think about him. The first thing I thought of was simple. It was to be delighted with him and to show him my delight. That in itself took us a good way towards becoming closer. Like some others of my close Co-Counsellors, B and I would not necessarily have become friends had we met outside of Co-Counselling. (Our ways of life are fairly different.) This sort of closeness involves commitment to the other person as they think about their life and make decisions to move forward in it. When I am listening to B in short Co-Counselling sessions on the phone, I am in a relaxed state of attention which doesn't contain any formed thoughts but is fully aware. I am not hoping for anything particular, I am just waiting to see what comes and trusting that I will know how to respond – if any active response is appropriate – just from my intelligent love for him.

Because we don't socialise I've had a chance to feel and discharge some particular old hurts. I have noticed some patterns surfacing in my relationship with B. They are old fears about closeness and feelings of possessiveness and insecurity. I mostly discharge on these feelings with other people, not with B, and I've succeeded in re-evaluating some old hurts by doing so. In general, I've noticed that my feelings for B, strong as they are, help me get closer to others, including my husband, which indicates to me that this sort of closeness is not distress but a contradiction to it.

Rachael: Because of conditioning to be a nurturing female, I have found myself drawn to offering male Co-Counsellors one-way attention. I'm not drawn to offering one-way time to other women. This is an example of how equal time structured into Co-Counsellling has helped me.

Regarding being peers, early on in Co-Counselling I would listen to my beloved clients and wonder why they were such 'basket cases'. Why couldn't they get their lives started and their problems solved? Later, as I learned about the characteristics of owning-class upbringings, I realised that arrogance and the assumption that I knew better were attitudes that I myself needed to discharge, and had nothing to do with the reality about my clients.

As a woman and a Jew, I have found certain classes of distresses easier to access. My mind will leap for those memories that bring tears because of feelings of victimisation (memories of the Holocaust, memories of physical abuse as a child and so on). Those distresses that have put me in the oppressor role in relation to other people are more difficult to see and grasp as distress. As an owning-class person, I feel more competent than other people, and it's hard for me to realise that this is a distress recording, and to access discharge on that. In our society, discharge is more likely to be supported when one is a victim.

I have a recent example of acting on logic. My husband lost his temper with our young children while I was out of town. The children called me, upset, and asked me to come home. I made contact with my husband over the phone, and he blamed me and the children for losing his temper. I felt like rushing home and shooting him! I felt more scared than the situation really called for. (The reason I felt so scared was that I had been the target of many lost tempers as a child.) I got as many Co-Counselling sessions as I could, discharged copiously, started to remember my husband's life story, and approached him with warmth and affection. As a result, he has apologised for his behaviour. Acting on my distressed feelings, I would have isolated him from me and the children. Not having done that, and having treated him humanly even though he made a mistake, makes it safer for everyone in the family to fall off the wagon without heavy blame coming at them.

Jenny: A close friend of mine has come to understand that if I'm crying, something good is happening and that it is helpful. I have found that he can listen more easily if the words I use while I'm crying are mostly about the goodness of reality. This actually helps me cry better, too. For example, if I am feeling upset about something in the present, I might ask if he can listen for a few minutes and say that I just need to cry. I'll look at him and say things like, 'You're my friend', 'Everything is OK', 'We love each other'. I've noticed that in this situation, and often in my Co-Counselling sessions, discharge goes better when I do this because I'm contradicting my hurt. Also, my friend is able to pay better attention when I'm not saying potentially restimulating things. I think on some level people realise that bad feelings most of the time have little to do with the present situation and they are relieved when that distinction is made. I used to think that being 'real' meant talking about my upsets with the current situation. As I discharge more of my early distresses, it becomes clear to me that what is actually being 'real' is expressing reality the way it really is – as something benign and good – and remembering that everyone is always doing his or her best, when everything is taken into account.

About appreciation and validation, I don't think I can remember a single criticism of myself that's been helpful to me. Whenever I, or anyone, is being criticised, it can only be that someone feels critical of our patterns, and our patterns are not our fault. Criticism is like adding insult to injury. I am behaving in an irritating way because I can't think clearly about something, because I was hurt. I'm trying as hard as I can not to act out this distress. This is true of everyone.

Emma: K has been my main Co-Counsellor for the past eleven years. I first came to know him because he taught an RC fundamentals class which I attended. I was still terribly hurt and scarred by the previous three years in the psychiatric system. I wanted to know more about RC, but I didn't feel I could show myself in any way. K was – he *is* – an incredibly gentle, kind and patient man. He let me hide away and not take part in games; he accepted that I didn't want to be part of any counselling demonstrations. He noticed that the way to engage me was in discussion, so he encouraged my questions. He even delighted in my cynicism. He discovered the things that interested me and asked me about them. He never pushed; he nudged, gently, and I still feel as though his hand is at my back, encouraging me forward. I was good at listening to other people, so I never struggled as a counsellor, but I struggled at being the client, and still do.

Back then I lived by a set of rigid rules. I suppose they were a set of patterns, and provided I lived within them, they offered me a feeling of safety. K gradually, with great gentleness, got me to tell him what the rules were, and then he patiently and repeatedly told me that there were no rules so there was no danger of breaking them. Things like talking about my feelings had been 'against the rules', as was any kind of touching – anything that might have brought some warmth into my life was against the rules. I know now that K hated the rules, but he never showed it back then! He always demonstrated his belief that I was doing the best I could do, and I respected him for that.

When I hurt my back, he was incredibly thoughtful. He counselled me on the pain, he dropped notes and little drawings through my letter box and the occasional tape to listen to. When he went abroad, supposedly forever, he asked if he could write to me. I agreed, although it was against my inner rules, which forbade ever getting attached to anyone and risking loss. Then someone told me he was ill, and he was coming back temporarily, and that he'd like to see me. I had to think about that because I was frightened that gaining him and losing him would be too much. I then made one of the most significant decisions in my whole life, one that blew my 'rules' wide apart. I decided that my relationship with K was worth taking risks for. I decided that I wanted to experience whatever was available to experience with him, for however long he would be here again, and that I would deal with 'losing him' when it happened. What made this most significant is that I had experienced so much death in my life, and that was partly why there were rules about not getting attached. At that time, there was a possibility that K might be so seriously ill that death was possible, but I wanted our relationship more than I was afraid of losing him.

So that was the first year of our relationship. It was somewhere during year two that I told K I had discharged enough that he could stop Co-Counselling with me now. I truly believed that he was counselling with me as a favour to me, to help me recover from the trauma of those years in the psychiatric system and the years that led up to them. It just wasn't within my comprehension that I might have been a good counsellor for him, that there might have been something in the relationship for him, too. We spent a few years working on that! I still struggle with it, but RC has taught me that what I feel and what is real are sometimes very different.

Those few years were amazing years in my life as a Co-Counsellor. K and I lived close together and really went with our Co-Counselling relationship. He had been an excellent teacher, and we always adhered to the no-socialising policy. It was so important for both of us to have that clear-cut boundary. It allowed us to push each other, and to push ourselves, to get close. We had phone contact most days, mostly for Co-Counselling, but quite often we had big discussions about RC theory that opened my life and my heart in astounding ways. Even though we have our struggles, I can't imagine anything, apart from death, breaking the relationship now.

We have been Co-Counselling for eleven years. K knows every single one of my deepest, darkest, most painful secrets – things I haven't yet found the courage to discharge about. But just knowing that someone else knows, and still respects and loves me, is enough to have shifted some of the fear and humiliation. He knows the things that hurt me and the things that bring me great joy. There's nothing I wouldn't or couldn't tell him. He and I both hold the real person in our hands and in our hearts, and the times when we can't see ourselves through all the bad feelings, we are there to give each other the true picture. And we know it has to be true, because we know each other in all our glory as well as in all our petty, snipey, unpleasant, bad moods.

Chapter 6

Hurts from oppression

As we find ways to discharge and eliminate all the patterns of racism, sexism, oppression of children, of nationalism, of oppression of physically disabled people, and all the other insidious viewpoints of oppression, it will become crystal clear to all of us that ALL MEN ARE SISTERS.

(Jackins 1993a: 108)

The beginnings of work on oppression in RC

I (Katie) began participating in Co-Counselling in 1968, relatively early in its history. I remember that at first there was no mention of hurts from oppression. However, in the early 1970s, some RC women – who at that time were participating in non-RC women's consciousness-raising groups – brought their new awareness of sexism into RC. If they were treated with less than full respect in a Co-Counselling session or RC group, they were no longer willing to accept it.

I remember an RC workshop near Seattle when this new awareness was gaining force. In their turns as clients before the group, first one woman, and then another and another, began crying and raging as they remembered instances of having been hurt by men. It turned into a lively and angry speak-out. For many of us, it was as if a light bulb had been turned on. Women who had never thought in these terms before, myself included, picked up the theme and used our turns to discharge about our hurts from sexism. We women knew something exciting and important was happening. We were like popcorn being freed from the pot! Righteous indignation and a sense of sisterhood blossomed.

Meanwhile, the men were mostly either cowering guiltily or showing the tense postures of defensiveness. A few men were so incensed that they walked out of the room and met together in one of the cabins. Male-female unity was not restored at this workshop – only later was it clarified that men are not, and should not be treated as, the 'enemy' – but this was a landmark event, and everyone knew it.

Awareness of sexism was growing in other parts of the RC Community as well, and it was an opportunity to think carefully about the kinds of hurts women were reacting to. It became clear that sexism was just one example of a class of hurts that happen to people because they belong to particular groups in society.

The first workshops specifically set up to focus on this topic were held in 1975. Various groups met together to explore this area. They met in separate caucuses to increase their awareness of the hurts they had suffered in common. Each group – women, Jews, Catholics, people of African heritage, young people, Gays and Lesbians, working-class people, people raised poor, people of Asian heritage, Indigenous people, Chicanos/as, Latinos/as – had a chance to speak about their experiences as members of those groups, first to each other and then to the larger group. The larger group was instructed to listen without argument or other verbal exchange, and learn.

At this point the Re-evaluation Counselling Communities adopted as a goal to include within them all oppressed sections of the population and to eliminate all racist, sexist, classist or other oppressive attitudes within the Communities. Oppression was precisely defined as *the systematic mistreatment of a group of people by the society and/or by another group of people who serve as agents of the society, with the mistreatment encouraged or enforced by the society and its culture.*

As this area of hurt was explored, it became evident that hurts from oppression constitute a large percentage of the hurts humans suffer. Tackling the hurts from sexism, racism, classism and so on is an integral part of helping humans regain their full selves and intelligence. After some discussion, the RC Communities took it on fully.

Nothing needed to be added to *basic* RC theory (which you've been reading about in this book) to accomplish the task. The solution was and is to discharge the hurts, by being listened to well by another human or humans. This began to happen in RC sessions and groups. However, hurts from oppression presented interesting challenges that required some new perspectives and some special formats to enable efficient discharge.

Distress recordings and oppression

One particularly useful point of RC theory for work on oppression is the recognition that *oppression can arise and operate only on the basis of distress recordings*. No human being would agree to submit to oppression unless a distress recording of submission had been installed previously while the human being was hurting. No human being would ever agree to, or participate in, oppressing another human being unless a distress recording had previously been installed through that person being hurt and then manipulated into the 'other end' of the pattern to play the role of the perpetrator of hurt or the role of the oppressor. Recordings of submission are almost always installed during childhood, so that our mistreatment as young people sets us up to accept subsequent oppressions. For example, a hurt recording from having been bullied has, as part of the recording, the role of bully and the role of recipient of bullying. When that recording is triggered, there will be a tendency to replay it in the bullying role, generally at someone unable to fight back. Not being able to defend oneself often relates to having less power in the society – so we see a white bully picking on a black person and getting away with it, or a parent abusing a child with the child having no recourse, a husband battering a wife who can't leave the situation for financial reasons, and so on.

Another example: a man frustrated by a demeaning and exploitative job may come home and take out his frustrations on his wife. He does so not only because he is hurting and not thinking, but also because his wife is a safe target. The proper target of his rage is the workplace, but if he expressed the depth of his rage and frustration at his boss or managers, or organised to improve the situation, he would be likely to lose his job. In turn, after being targeted, the woman is predictably upset and may take it out on her children – and the hurt is passed on. Hurts can be and are inflicted in the opposite direction (from the woman to the man), but the power differential in society invites and reinforces the direction of the mistreatment as indicated.

Unique features and challenges

Hurts from oppression have some unique features. Oppression is ingrained in and reinforced by society. Everyone who has grown up in a particular society has been immersed in, and hurt by, the various kinds of systematic mistreatment. Since early in our lives, we have been bombarded with false messages about other groups of people, as well as about the groups we ourselves belong to. This poses a particular challenge for discharging these hurts.

As you may recall, discharge occurs spontaneously when we can notice that our hurt, or hurt recording, does not represent present-time reality. How do we achieve discharge when oppression is apparently the present-time reality all around us? How do we contradict the hurt sufficiently if both client and counsellor are so conditioned as to be almost unaware of it? How can we be effective counsellors for each other when the counsellor is from a group that has played the perpetrator role (for example, a white Co-Counsellor) and the client is in the oppressed role (for example, a black Co-Counsellor) or vice versa? We had to work out ways to get enough of a view outside of these hurts – enough contradiction, enough grasp of what the world is or could be like without oppression – to effectively discharge them. We have devised many perspectives and formats to meet the challenge.

Discharging on having been oppressed

We have found it useful for oppressed and oppressor groups to first meet separately and discharge on their respective common hurts within the safety of that commonality. (Once the safety has been achieved, these new understandings can be shared with the larger group.)

When members of an oppressed group speak out about their oppression, they typically discharge and re-evaluate. Those listening try to avoid being restimulated and to learn. The RC context facilitates empathy and hearing what is being said. People share specific instances of having been put down, discriminated against, and otherwise treated as less than human. They usually show their vulnerability and discharge as they speak, and this tends to reach and move the listeners and to cause them to want to help end that form of mistreatment. Listeners are also motivated to discharge their own patterns that have made life difficult for these brothers and sisters.

I (Katie) remember being astounded by the way such speak-outs added a whole new dimension to my Co-Counsellors. My awareness of one of my Co-Counsellors was limited to liking her a lot and knowing something about her struggles. When she realised the implications of having been raised working class, she was tremendously excited and relieved. Up to that time, she had thought certain hurts were just personal to her, and it was a great eye-opener to discover that other working-class people had been hurt in similar ways. She was now able to take this mistreatment less personally and thus avoid being restimulated by it. A clearer understanding that her hurts from classism were not her fault made it easier to discharge them. She worked in sessions on how her father's exhausting blue-collar job had had an impact on him and therefore on her family. She realised that some of the tense ways he behaved at home were directly related to his job. This made it possible to see him in a different light and to treat him more lovingly. These changes meant more contradiction to her hurts, and she had easier access to discharge. She was also discharging in RC working-class support groups. I watched her become stronger, less deferential – actually very powerful – and a strong advocate for the working class, both in RC and outside of it.

In Co-Counselling sessions with me she sometimes described how oppressive middle-class culture had been to her and her friends – in school, in jobs and elsewhere. Oops! *I* was middle-class (though I had barely thought about it at that point), so it wasn't always easy to listen to her grief and anger about middle-class patterns. However, as she discharged, I realised that some of my middle-class conditioning not only made her life more difficult but also did not serve me well. I had good Co-Counselling sessions about it. I had these sessions with other middle-class people, so that she would not have to listen to my distress in this area. (RC figured out that it reinforces the oppression if members of the oppressed group have to listen to the group that oppressed them talk about that oppression.) A whole new world opened up to me. I gained new appreciation for working-class people and ever since have wanted to make friends across class lines. Before, I would not have had the clear thinking to do this. My life has been better for it.

The oppressor role

At first RC focused most attention on hurts from being in the oppressed role and on strategies for discharging these hurts. There were many speak-outs at RC workshops. People in the non-targeted (oppressor) roles listened, learned, tried to behave better and felt guilty. Something additional was needed.

As we worked in this area, it became clear that both roles are rooted in early hurts. People are literally forced into the oppressor role. We wouldn't discriminate against another group without having first been hurt ourselves. Anyone acting oppressively toward a group of people has to have been *hurt into* not thinking clearly about that group.

As soon as they were given some space to think about it, male Co-Counsellors were eager to talk about how they had been hurt as boys and men. Women listened, and the men listened to each other. Soon there was no question but that boys and men have been systematically hurt. The agent of the oppression in this case is social institutions and attitudes rather than a particular group. The mistaken attitudes have, for example, caused men to be singled out for harsher mistreatment if they discharge: they are not supposed to cry or be scared. Boys are not generally held and nurtured in the same way girls are. Co-Counsellors have had to get rid of such attitudes and beliefs to be helpful counsellors to men. In addition, specific institutions are particularly hurtful to men, such as the armed services and the workplace. Men are required to be ready to fight for their nation or group, to kill or be killed in the name of manhood. This readiness does not come naturally to male humans but requires mistreatment as preparation. Men's bodies tend to be treated as disposable in other ways, as when they are allocated the most dirty and dangerous work (Irwin *et al.* 1992; Jackins *et al.* 1999).

It has become completely clear that blame and guilt serve no useful purpose. This has been an important perspective for discharging the hurts of both the oppressed and oppressor roles.

In recent years the RC Communities have focused much attention on discharging the oppressor role, particularly in terms of white racism. An RC project, United to End Racism, was initiated in 2001 to promote discharge on racism and to take knowledge of how to do this outside of the RC Communities (see Appendix 1 for a fuller description of United to End Racism).

Internalised oppression

Oppression becomes *internalised*. Members of an oppressed group turn the invalidation and discrimination that they have individually felt from the oppressors on themselves and on each other. Realising this was a breakthrough. The Re-evaluation Counselling concept of internalised oppression has become widely used outside of RC, usually without awareness of its origins.

Here is an example of internalised women's oppression. At the college where I (Caroline) work, the senior management is almost entirely male, and they are quite unaware of sexism. Recently I, and some women colleagues, protested about discrimination in the way appointments were made. We got nowhere. When the news came, I felt as if I had thrown myself at a solid wall and been knocked back, winded and humiliated. Then came my internalised oppression ('We *must* be inferior, or this couldn't be happening'), as I and my female colleagues tried to work out what *we* had done 'wrong'. We blamed ourselves.

My internalised oppression can take other forms. It can seem that the stereo-types about women apply to other women but not to me. *Other* women are overly emotional, limited in their vision and compulsive caretakers of others. They weakly allow themselves to be taken advantage of – but *I* am an adventurous, powerful, strong woman! Being committed to women's liberation has not prevented me from sometimes having contemptuous feelings about other women.

I also carry another set of distress recordings from internalised oppression: I feel I am *less of a woman* than other women. As a girl I was sometimes told I wasn't pretty and feminine (so I'd better be clever, nice and funny). I didn't look 'right', and everyone knows that an attractive appearance is crucial to being a successful woman. Both 'inferior' and 'superior' forms of internalised oppression are equally divisive and debilitating. I'd been Co-Counselling for several years before I noticed that 'beautiful' women were just as badly hurt as I was and carried just as much internalised oppression. Their recordings might be different, for example, 'My entire value is in my appearance, and this is all anyone will ever love about me.'

What I've described applies equally to other oppressed groups. I have often heard disabled people say, 'I don't like being with other disabled people; I can't stand them' – internalised oppression. I've seen men unable to think of anything at all, however small, that they like about other men – internalised oppression. I've heard former mental patients express their shame at having been shut up 'with all those loonies' – internalised oppression.

We can think of a thousand reasons to blame ourselves and others. Our heads are full of images of times when we held back because of fear or when we did or said all the wrong things. We often feel as if we have disappointed, betrayed or hurt people we love, and we blame ourselves. We may also feel bitterness, resentment and shame remembering occasions when we were used, cheated or treated like objects. That this happened seems to prove we really are worthless. We are not usually encouraged to understand these feelings in terms of socially enforced mistreatment. Without this understanding, we are set adrift, prey to false explanations for our difficulties. Without an accurate explanation, we can't figure out how to change our lives in crucial areas or efficiently discharge the hurts we've suffered.

It has become clear that we are not to blame for the effects of oppression. This phenomenon existed long before we did. It overwhelmed and overpowered us as young people, even though we fought against it as hard and as long as we could. 'Fortunately . . . neither internalized oppression nor the impulse to oppress others is part of any of our genes. Rather, oppression has imposed these patterns. Because they are not inherent, they may be overcome and eliminated' (Roby 1998: 31).

Questions about oppression

We got together with Gillian, Neil and Emma, who are all working class, and asked them a series of questions which are sometimes used in workshops to help people think about oppression and so that others may learn. (Any other group may be substituted for working class.)

What's been good about being working class?

- People look after each other to a certain extent. Where I was brought up, you still don't go to somebody's wake without a bit of food.
- Working-class people have good access to their humour. It's often vulgar humour but really funny. We've got this way of being together in a group and having a good time.
- Where I live, people trust me, I think because I understand struggle. I like being able to have a good time, and laugh.

What's been hard about being working class?

- It was hard growing up quite poor. It wasn't deprivation; we had enough to eat and enough clothes to wear, but it was basic. For me, something that sums up being working class is being in a comic shop when I was 9 with my dad, and he says I can have one comic. There are seven that I want, and I know he's being really good; my mum wouldn't let me have even one. What a choice! It's not real deprivation, but as a child, it feels like it. That's why if I'm in a comic shop or a CD shop now, I just buy whatever I want. It's also to do with confidence. There's a confidence you have from a certain background or a certain amount of money, that was certainly missing from my working-class home, and sometimes I see that my children, too, hold themselves back, and I think, 'How did that get in?'
- I was poorly educated. Working-class girls had three options: to work in a local factory, be a hairdresser, or be a nurse. I didn't even know I could go into further education. My lack of education meant I felt stupid. When I was a child, the hardest thing was that my mum had to work, so I just never knew her really.
- I've got some resentment that it was just expected that after I left school I would go out and get a job temporarily, until I got married. I'd have loved to go to college, to have had that independence. I didn't feel comfortable around people who were clever or intellectual, because I knew so little. Assumptions can still be hard. People sometimes assume, because I look a particular way and have a South London accent, that I'm a 'dumb blonde' and there's nothing to me. There's this chap in the village; every time he saw me he would say, 'Oh hello little Gilly!' I met him at a party and I said 'I may be little, but I bite!' He's stopped doing it now.

What do you like about other working-class people?

- They speak their minds. My experience of working-class people is that they're genuine and real. I know where I am with them.

- My life is driven by social services and state benefits. I always know when somebody from the benefits agency is working class, because they're more human about it. When they decided to stop paying me housing benefit, the woman sat at my computer and wrote a three-page letter of complaint. I could tell she was working class. There's a warmth there.

- Thinking of my job, working-class people are good at relating, at working together and getting along.

What can't you stand about other working-class people? (This question is worded to reveal the internalised oppression.)

- I can't stand the powerlessness, hopelessness, violence, addictions – in other words, I can't stand seeing the effects of the oppression.

- Our family was completely fractured. We were a big family but there wasn't much connection. I was sent to live with my Nan.

- I hate the low expectations working-class people often have for children.

What do you never want to hear said again about working-class people?

- That they're the 'salt of the earth'. I hate the sentimentalising.

- I don't like stereotyping of working-class people, the idea that we are thugs or whores. You've got to know someone to love them, and if you go around thinking all working-class people are thugs or slags, you never will get to know them.

- I don't like that saying that we live in a 'classless society', because we don't. And I don't like the attitude when someone does something that's unacceptable: 'Oh, what do you expect?' Meaning, because they're working class.

How have you been able to use RC to recover from working-class internalised oppression?

- RC has been a place where I could practise taking leadership and being visible, a sort of training ground for me to do it in the world. To do this I had to discharge the feelings of stupidity and worthlessness that were put on me by the oppression. It's still hard for me to be a visible leader outside of RC, but now I can do it.

- I led the local working-class group for a couple of years. We were thinking about how to make RC welcoming to working-class people. That work made me more confident. It's made it easier for me to deal with other people's class patterns. Now I'm leading the local RC leaders' group and we've been working on class for more than a year, because there used to be a class divide in this RC Community. People are getting much closer and being more honest.

- Because of Co-Counselling, I've been able to put myself in situations where I have to speak up and make myself heard. I've also had opportunities to lead, and leading is much better for me than participating because it contradicts my feelings of insignificance. When I do start talking I realise I know much more than I used to think I knew.

The following questions may also be useful: When did you first realise you were a member of a particular group? What was happening? Can you remember any of the following – being criticised, put down, dismissed, ignored, hated, hating, feeling uncomfortable, being numb, feeling superior or inferior, feeling angry, powerless, isolated, bored, stupid, or anything else that you attribute to having been a member of that group? Who treated you this way? Members of your own group? People not part of your group? Both? The society in general? Do you remember noticing someone else being oppressed? Do you recall a hurtful incident that installed a recording that made it possible for you to play an oppressor role?

Experience-sharing

Ebony: Messages from the oppressions of being black, being poor, being black and poor, and living on a small farm in the rural US South were already deeply ingrained in my people when I was born. Feeling ugly and ashamed and bad about myself, feeling like I didn't have a place, came in early and hard, and the messages from the racism and classism reinforced each other. They worked hand-in-hand to leave me with hurts that even now startle me with their messages. Recently the feeling of being ugly, that I keep at bay, hit with force. I walked around feeling 'excruciatingly ugly'. I discharged a bunch on this feeling, knowing it was one of my earliest feelings about myself and knowing it was the internalised hatred from racism. I had internalised the racist messages that the 'acceptable' look was white. I did not have the physical characteristics of white people. My hair was not straight or 'good'. We called it 'nappy'. Beginning as a young person and lasting for many decades, I worried about how to get my hair longer and thicker and looking more 'acceptable'. When I was growing up, I used a hot comb to straighten my hair (like most black females). Later, I used chemical hair relaxers. One day, after I had been Co-Counselling for a few years, the question popped into my mind, 'Who are you trying to look like?' I became eager to know what my hair looked and felt like without the effort to straighten it.

Being targeted for a visible characteristic – the colour of my skin – has had me walk around every day very conscious of people's reactions to me. It's like a tape that is never turned off. I am subject, at any time, to being the target of aware or unaware racism. I don't know what it's like to not have this heightened awareness that continually leaves some part of my mind and attention on racism. What I would love most would be to be a human in the world and go about enjoying all other humans without any hint of any oppression.

I attended segregated schools. It was a fact that the newest books went to the white school. The white school was better than the black school. Even though I graduated at the top of my class, I devalued my status and felt I had just been lucky to make it.

Some of the racism that has come at me has been subtle, some shrouded in a blanket of pretence, some overt and some unaware (if one would call 'unaware' the mindset that this is how a person who is not white should be treated). White co-workers have not acknowledged me when we've accidentally met in a public place away from the work environment. A white person looked with disdain at my being his seatmate on an airplane and then left the seat for the rest of the trip. I've been followed in stores as though I would steal. I've been ignored or passed over while waiting in line to purchase items. Three white young men threatened to run me over with a truck when I was walking on the side of a country road. A white woman harangued me on a bus, telling me to move away from her. White people take a tighter grip on their purses or cross the street when I'm approaching.

Every institution perpetuates racism. The justice system, the courts, the educational system and the 'mental health' system have been particularly detrimental to my people. Prisons are becoming the new plantations. Young black children are treated as though they are stupid, can't learn and have 'problems' that need to be controlled with medication.

Emma: We're all caught up in this oppressive system in which disabled people aren't even supposed to *be*. Most of the resources that disabled people need to live their lives are being put toward finding the 'solution' – be that 'curing' us or finding ways to eradicate disabled foetuses. I'm invisible. I don't exist. I'm not being thought about at all. Disabled people have been invisible for generation after generation. In my lifetime disabled people have been disposable, put into institutions and forgotten about. No one has ever really known what to do about us, other than to shut us away somewhere so that we don't exist.

What is happening now is that our own homes have become the institutions, where no one has to know of our existence. I'm even more invisible than I would have been forty years ago, high on a hill away from everyone else. At least then people knew about 'that place', even if they felt uncomfortable and uneasy and not right about it. This way, with me being institutionalised in my own home, no one sees me, I don't exist. Problem solved. A bunch of people who restimulate such awful feelings are so much easier to continue to ignore.

As a disabled person in the world, I spend almost every moment of my life witnessing oppressive behaviour. It's exhausting and frustrating to depend upon agencies that aren't designed to function, so that the people who work for the agencies are very stressed. These agencies control my finances, my healthcare, my home life. I have to fill in forms that detail how many times a day I need to use the toilet, for how long each time, and what help I need. It's a humiliating, demoralising experience, and were it not for the knowledge I have through my use of RC, I would have yielded to the oppression long ago. Had I done so, I would be living in squalor, very ill, with not enough money to exist on.

Because I'm disabled, I have to work hard to sustain relationships with people. I didn't used to bother, or would give up entirely. The difficulty is that other people are making mistakes all the time and I have to make the decision to tell them, knowing that I'm going to have to put my own feelings aside and pursue these people. Usually they feel completely humiliated that I've noticed they're behaving in a strange or oppressive way. They had no idea. They can get angry or disappear completely. I have to be in 'counselling mode' a lot of the time, and it gets exhausting. Sometimes I get completely caught up in the oppression and feel worthless, and I get very alone and isolated. I'm so used to losing people that I find it hard to love them in the first place, so to keep loving them is tough.

It's easy to love people who see beyond their feelings of ineptness around me – younger people, or people who I've come to know over the Internet who got to know the *me* part of me before they got to know that I happen to be disabled. It's hard when you can't hide the thing that makes people behave in ways that range from odd to abusive. I used to not use my wheelchair, just so people would connect with me. Conversely, when children are involved, I know that my wheelchair is going to guarantee my appeal, because they love to investigate it and take parts off and see what each lever does.

Someone just reminding me that they like me can be an enormous thing, because the nature of the oppression of disabled people is that you're not wanted. When you're faced with oppression like this most of the time, it can be really easy to forget that it's not about any one person – me or anyone else.

I want to say something about mental health oppression as well. I was in a mental hospital for three years, off and on, in my twenties. I was depressed, I couldn't bear being at home and I'd tried to kill myself a few times. In the hospital one of the nurses would hug me. That was an amazing feeling. I used to write it in a diary. This nurse left. Because I was very upset, they diagnosed me as having a 'dependent personality disorder'. Now there's this mark on my health record, 'personality disorder' – I've seen it on my file in great big red letters, and it's affected everything. When I first hurt my back, it was 'a physical manifestation of a psychiatric disorder'. Luckily, the general practitioner believed that I was in pain and insisted on sending me to hospital. They still wanted to send me back, and she said, 'You *are* keeping her in hospital!', which they did, and they found there was something physically wrong. But it was only because she believed me.

I'm afraid I could go there tomorrow with a brain tumour and they would just see 'personality disorder' and that's what they would 'treat'. And this is fifteen years on. It got better for a while because when the files were paper it got further and further back, but then they went computerised, so now if I went to see any doctor in England they'd tap in my details on the computer and they'd bring up 'psychiatric illness – personality disorder' and that's what they'd 'treat' me for.

Rachael: Co-Counselling has been most useful to me in giving me a context for my hurts. The context is anti-Jewish oppression. With this context I have been able to see how being hurt as Jews forced my parents to mistreat me the exact way they did, forced my sister and me into the difficulties we have, and forced me into a life of competition, insecurity and frenetic activity. Under that kind of pressure, anyone (because we're all inherently these ways) would have ended up brilliant, successful and admired – and I was and am! Those things are supposed to bring happiness, but much of the enjoyment of life has eluded me. For example, have I ever lain on my back in a field and looked at the clouds?

In this society, Jews are the target of blame for the ills of the world. The common phrases are, 'They own the media', 'They own the banks', with the implication that the gross unfairness of the capitalist system is caused by greedy Jews. One thing I've understood from Co-Counselling is that it's in the interest of the oppressive society to offer people groups toward which they can target their upset feelings, with the approval of the society as a whole. Targeting another group is a great relief valve for people's terrible feelings and effectively prevents people from challenging the structures of the society. Let me explain. The economy gets tight, you lose your job. Whose fault is it anyway? Aha! Those greedy Jews that own the banks! Your friends will agree. The media will support you. Literature through the ages, from Shakespeare to the present, will offer stereotypes that support this perspective. How can you possibly get your mind free to notice that the powers-that-be benefit from your upset at Jews? This upset prevents you from actively organising to change policies of large corporations that pay managers ever more expansively and workers ever more wretchedly. They take their business to other countries, and we lose jobs here. This targeting of Jews will prevent you from noticing that the line-up in political, corporate and financial power is overwhelmingly white, male and Gentile.

Kerry: As an Irish person in England, after several years I became quite frustrated with English behaviour. It came as a relief to decide that the strange actions and attitudes of which I was on the receiving end were due to English people having been hurt in ways I hadn't been, and to decide as an Irish man that I could take charge of my relationships with English people. This decision not to be a victim to oppression has had a powerful effect on my sessions and in the rest of my life.

Neil: I think Gay oppression is used to keep men and women in gender roles and to keep sexism intact. As a parent of a boy, I've noticed how quickly and early Gay stuff is used to bring children, especially boys and parents, into line. People will make remarks about the colour of clothes or choice of toys. I remember at a party, when my son was 1 year old, he kissed the little boy beside him and someone said, 'Oh, you'll need to keep an eye on him' and made a limp wrist gesture. It's clear to me that any attempt to step outside the allotted gender role is quickly squashed – usually by jokes, but the implication is clear that you will be ostracised or excluded – and it works to inhibit people.

Gay oppression is especially vicious in how it creates isolation. Unlike with many other oppressed groups, there is no sense of belonging to a group or having a kindred identity with your family. Most young Gay people experience terrible isolation from friends and family. The targeting starts very young and is so effective that it isn't a coincidence that it's difficult to find heterosexual allies. Most heterosexuals have seen what the oppression is like and know that if they stand up for Gay people, they will be targeted. I've worked with some heterosexual allies in Co-Counselling, and they are scared. In some ways they are more scared than Gay people. Gay people have had the experience of dealing with the oppression and mostly surviving.

The sense of being different, of being bad, of not being wanted, is central to Gay oppression and is a key distress for Gay people. It sometimes manifests itself in a determination to be different at all costs. I once counselled a Gay man who never wore ordinary trousers but always wore baggy coloured pantaloons. He took enormous pride in this, and many of his counsellors congratulated him on his exotic and colourful clothes sense. I counselled him on buying and wearing an ordinary pair of jeans, and the distress that came up for discharge was amazing.

Gay people are hurt daily by vicious remarks. We are a group about whom it is still OK to make derogatory remarks. People who wouldn't dream of using offensive words to describe black people or women won't see a problem with 'pouf' or 'pansy'. I just have to hear one of those words casually dropped into the conversation and my stomach turns in fear and my brain stops.

Gay people are attacked and killed for no other reason than their being Gay, and the legal system is usually quite lenient, especially if the Gay man made a pass – then clearly he deserved to die. When it comes to custody, courts regularly take children away from Lesbian mothers.

I could go on and on. Even simple things like reading a list of oppressed groups with no mention of Gay oppression is heartbreaking. It shouldn't matter, but it does. It feels as if as Gay people we have to constantly fight alone for our rights, fight to be recognised or heard or taken seriously. It does make us over-sensitive and defensive, but we have been a targeted group for centuries. Having a few more bars and clubs doesn't make us liberated.

Despair is a key part of Gay oppression – I think we really do feel deep down that no one will help, that no one cares, that no will stand up for us, that we are truly alone. Not the easiest distress in the world to deal with, especially if it has a coating of cynicism and defensiveness.

From the age of 14, I was picked on at school for being Gay. It horrified me that people could see it. I felt, and still feel to some degree, that there is a big neon sign above my head flashing '*pouf*'! My best friend and I were both targeted, but we never discussed it, and I found out years later that he was Gay as well. It seems so sad that we weren't able to tell each other. For me, the fear that he, too, would turn against me kept me from mentioning anything.

For about five years I was 'out' as Gay in my workplace and it was liberating. Careerwise it was a disaster – almost overnight my work was seen as second-rate. It wasn't anything you could argue with, you just knew the managers' prejudices were in full swing. The people I worked with were great, and I certainly felt for the first time as if all of me was present at work.

Now that I'm married and have children, most people assume I'm hetero-sexual, and I find myself feeling back in the closet again. I don't want to be open about my Gay past in case people run their prejudices at my children. I'm back in a position of hiding some part of me again. On a silly level, it's about being careful not to be too enthusiastic about Barbra Streisand or Bette Davis. On a deeper level, it's about losing a part of myself again or locking a part of me away. I think that's the real hurt of Gay oppression.

Gillian: Being white is the first example that came to mind of how I've been hurt by an oppression that didn't target me. When I was 14 or 15 I had an experi-ence which will stay with me forever, and which really had an impact on my relationships with black people and other people of colour. I used to go away on camps in the summer holidays with a religious youth group. I loved these camps, as I had contact with lots of different young people whom I wouldn't usually get a chance to hang out with. On one camp my friend and I made friends with a young Afro-Caribbean boy. We kept in touch for a few months, and at Christmas time that year he sent me a present. I was so delighted and thrilled that I showed my mum the bottle of perfume I'd been given and then proudly picked out in the group photo the young boy who had sent it to me. She immediately said I should send it back. I felt confused and upset and actually refused to send it back, but I never wrote to that boy again. I knew then that something wasn't right, but I felt powerless to do anything about it. That incident gave me the message that I shouldn't have relationships with black people. I think the experience was supposed to leave me feeling superior to this lovely young boy I had met, but all I felt was loss, confusion, isolation and powerlessness. This was the early experience that always came up when I worked on racism with other white people in RC. I'm no longer willing to accept this separation. Recently I have been making close relationships with black people, and I have started an RC support group for white people working on eliminating racism.

Caroline: As a white person I haven't been targeted by racism, but I've certainly been hurt by it. There is a big difference between the way racism hurts black people — who may be killed, made poor, insulted, harassed or excluded because of it — and the way it hurts me. But my hurt is real, too. It is hurtful to human beings to be in an oppressor role. If I stop to notice, I can see that my life is narrower and poorer because of racism. Racism has disconnected me from most of the world's population, from all sorts of beauty and knowledge. It's made me hurtful, as well as clumsy, awkward and ignorant. I want equal access to all the world's peoples as friends, partners, teachers, colleagues.

I've worked on the misinformation I received as a young person, which still affects me. I can go to Gillian's support group, and discharge about the false and stereotypic images of people of colour I've seen in films, on television and in stories and comic books. I can work on the first time I noticed that differences of skin colour were considered important. I can work on my own relationships with black people. I can discharge my regrets at the losses and the misunderstandings. I can apologise for the mistakes. I can appreciate the successes. I can experiment with phrases such as 'I am a white person, no better than any black person'. I can work on what I admire about black people and on what I fear and dislike. I can work on my feelings about white people. I can work for a just world in which resources are equally shared. I was set up to be racist at the time I was born by the accident of skin colour. It's not my fault, but I am responsible for getting rid of it. If I hadn't been oppressed myself as a young person, I would never have been numb to racism, played it out, or found it acceptable to be privileged at someone else's expense. I can reject it completely.

I want to say something about the oppression of middle-class people as well. Because middle-class people tend to be reasonably well off, and are often in positions of authority — inadvertently participating in the mistreatment of working-class people — many people don't realise that we, too, have been systematically mistreated. From our earliest days middle-class children are given confusing messages about ourselves and the world, and are told that we are mistaken about our own experiences. (My mum often told me that I didn't feel what I felt!) The love we are offered tends to be conditional on being good and doing the right thing. These are severe hurts, and their effects on adult middle-class people are apparent — we are often confused about the world, we become fixated on appearances, on pleasing others, or obeying authority. I vividly remember the moment when, as an 11-year-old in a mainly working-class school, I won a scholarship to a privileged private secondary school. I was upset at the separation from my friends and at their resentment, but seduced by the praise I received. That was just one moment in a long process that happened to me and other middle-class people: being bribed and threatened into believing that we are somehow different from, and better than, working-class people, and becoming separated and disconnected not only from them but also, to a large extent, from each other and from ourselves. A lot of what I've done in RC is to get back that sense of connection with all people.

Daire: The groups I am conscious of belonging to or having belonged to are male, young, middle-class, Irish, heterosexual, raised-Catholic, fundamentalist Christian, atheist and white.

When I was a child, a friend of my father stayed with us for a weekend. I was extremely fond of this man. He was affectionate, funny, and always had time for me. One Sunday morning when I got up to go to Mass, I noticed that he was still in bed. I asked my mother about this, and she explained that he was not Catholic. I'm not sure what messages I had been exposed to up to this point, but it was only then that I first saw their effect. My reaction to hearing that he wasn't Catholic was one of surprise – something along the lines of, 'But he's such a nice man!' This was my first experience of a non-Catholic person, and I had already picked up an association of non-Catholicism with heretics and generally shady characters. In meeting such a pleasant non-Catholic man, I felt disappointed and somewhat indignant that I had been misled into these myths about non-Catholics, but I didn't know what to do about it.

I've got an example of gender oppression. At lunchtime in my primary school, the boys would invariably go around the back of the school to play soccer while the girls stayed around the front playing various less athletic games. For a period of a few days in sixth class (when I was 12 or so), I decided I didn't want to play soccer and wound up spending lunchtime with the girls, playing 'Ship Deck Shore' or some such game. On returning to the classroom after lunch, I was greeted with suspicion from the boys, who interrogated me on how I had spent lunch and regarded my answers dubiously. More than anything else I was surprised by this gender segregation, and to this day I'm still a little startled.

An experience to do with my oppression as a young person occurred at the end of an RC workshop. I was approaching the front door of the building in which the workshop was being held, when I noticed a lady behind me with a large suitcase (not an RCer – there was some other group using the building as well). She was still a long way from the door, but both it and her suitcase appeared unwieldy, so I decided to wait and hold the door for her. Once she was outside, she set down the suitcase and said, 'Would you put that on the bus for me?' I was somewhat annoyed by her impoliteness but helped her with the bag anyway, which earned me a 'good boy' (I was 17 at the time). I can forgive her rudeness – sometimes people just are like that – but what bothered me was the assumption that politeness was not required on account of me being many years her junior. Another thought: it is said that young people should not vote because they wouldn't understand the implications of their voting and would undermine the democratic process with trivial or ignorant votes, but the very same arguments were made when women first sought the right to vote.

Jenny: A Co-Counsellor who does a lot of work with children noticed that if a child is about to hit another child and can be stopped before doing the hitting, he or she will often be able to discharge. If no one can intervene in time, and the child goes ahead and hits the other child, it's difficult for the hitting child to discharge and recover. That child knows that he or she has done something wrong, and this has an inhibiting effect on the discharge. Also, all the sympathy goes to the child who was hit, and the child doing the hitting is often isolated, disapproved of, made to feel guilty and punished.

One has to have first been hurt or oppressed to be carrying out the hurting or oppressor role. Then there is the additional hurt of hurting another human and being isolated for it. I think it will help if we understand that any 'oppressor' was initially hurt, and that the acting out of oppression on others is hurtful to the oppressor, too. Assisting the person in the oppressor role to stop acting it out is clearly good not only for the people he or she has been oppressing, but for himself or herself as well.

Katie: I'd like to connect the information from the above 'speak-outs' with being effective counsellors and clients. Information like this can help us avoid unintentionally reinforcing people's hurts. It might be a useful exercise to review each of these stories and think of something you would never say to each person because it would reinforce his or her oppression. Then think of a way to show caring. Can you think of something you could say to each one that might validate and reassure them and give them a picture of the reality outside the oppression they have suffered? If you are caring and accurate (and if you had a chance to counsel them), they would likely start discharging the hurts they have been describing. Then imagine that you are the client being counselled by Emma, or Ebony, or Neil and the others in our 'class'. What might you need to be sensitive to, with each, as you were talking about your own hurts? Next, you can begin the process of completely eliminating your potential for unaware behaviour by having sessions in which you talk about the thoughts and feelings you noticed as you read each story. Beyond that, you might consider making friends with someone you would like to get to know who is a member of a group mentioned above that may previously have seemed off-limits to you.

Chapter 7

Stories

Mansour's story: many years, many changes

Mansour: I was introduced to Re-evaluation Counselling in 1975 when I was a 20-year-old undergraduate student at the University of California at San Diego. I had spoken as a male ally at a women's liberation event, and news of the event appeared in the campus newspaper. My first RC teacher was shown a copy by a mutual friend and invited me to come talk with her. All I knew was that she was teaching a class on 'human liberation' and was interested in having me participate. Little did I know what a major turning point this would be in my life.

Growing up in a working-class family in Los Angeles, all I knew about 'liberation' was what my mother had told me about being Catholic – that we didn't believe in racism or the oppression of Jews ('we are all children of God') and that we were for the poor. As a boy, it bothered me to hear about violence and hunger in the world, and I dreamed of being able to do something to make a difference. At a personal level, I loved my family, and it was painful to see their struggles with money, tranquillisers, alcoholism, depression and the 'mental health' system. I tried to help them by making them happy and not causing trouble, but it was hard keeping all my own feelings inside and living such an isolated life.

By the time I was 14 I was thinking about how I could escape. At 18, I finally left home to go to college. Unfortunately, as a low-income student at an upper-middle-class university, I felt more isolated than ever, as though I were from another planet. I knew I needed help with the loneliness and depression but didn't want to seek psychological counselling out of fear that it would go on my record. In 1975 I became aware of progressive politics for the first time and committed myself to making a better world. All the misinformation I had absorbed in the United States was challenged and my view of the world was shaken up. It was a process of seeing systemic injustice clearly for the first time and connecting it to my own background and experience. I was full of intense feelings with no one to talk to about them.

One of the first things I heard about Co-Counselling was that someone would exchange listening time with me, and for an hour I would get to talk about anything I wanted to talk about. I was amazed and intrigued by this idea. It seemed that no one had ever listened to me, let alone for an hour – and certainly not about anything I wanted! After twenty-seven years I still treasure this opportunity to receive caring attention from another human being as I share and sort through my various thoughts and feelings. It is also enormously satisfying to do the same for others and thus make a profound difference for us both.

Fortunately, I was able to discharge easily from the beginning, even before learning theory in class. One day while reading the literature about how to counsel, I came up with a phrase that made me cry. It was 'My daddy died'. (My father had passed away from cirrhosis when I was 8 years old.) I cried heavily about our relationship and this early loss for countless hours over a long period – in Co-Counselling sessions, classes, workshops and support groups. It was a great relief. The old feelings of depression began to lift, and life and relationships looked completely different. I knew I would stick with this process all the way and wanted nothing more than to make these tools available to everyone in the world.

I became part of the local RC Community and was given the job of librarian of RC books and journals. During breaks from school I would spend days in my apartment reading everything from cover to cover. Although I still struggled with the old isolation, my hopes of overcoming it and other patterns increased enormously as I read the ideas and experiences of this worldwide community.

Many men in this society have difficulties showing feelings and discharging our grief through tears. I've wondered what allowed me to keep this channel of recovery open. It may have to do with my family's cultural background, which is Lebanese and Italian. My family was emotional and expressed feelings easily. Although this was often beneficial, the way it was done was sometimes terrifying and humiliating. I felt ashamed to cry and feared being ridiculed. After keeping it all inside for most of my life, RC gave the permission I needed to let go in a safe atmosphere. Still it was difficult for me to shake and discharge heavy fear, to give up the calm exterior I had relied on for survival. Whenever I tried, it seemed like I was faking it. Then much later, during a period of unemployment when I spent a lot of time alone in my apartment, I found that the only way to stop pacing nervously was to plant myself in front of the mirror and shake. It still felt unreal, but I noticed my body turning different temperatures and vibrating, so I decided something was going on. At last I became able to do more shaking and can tell that it has relaxed me.

During my early years in RC I did a lot of counselling about my family, how much I loved them, and the hard experiences we had gone through. Then after about five to ten years, I found it difficult to keep discharging. I would talk about the same things but without much emotion. I began to have feelings of needing my counsellors to be different or more skilful or more aware. I sought such counsellors in my RC Community, at RC workshops, and through correspondence with Harvey Jackins. Despite the support I received, it never seemed enough, and I went through many sessions discharging in small amounts but not heavily. The most important thing I did at this stage was to persist. I knew that little by little I would get enough discharge and re-evaluation to figure out how to make faster progress.

Then I began reading articles in *Present Time* about closeness and noticing the presence of one's counsellor. Up to this point I had not looked at my counsellor much but told stories of people from the past while looking away from the person I was with in the present. I began spending more time in sessions noticing my Co-Counsellor, what was true about her or him and our relationship, and letting it sink in that I wasn't alone. My 'dry spell' ended and I began discharging copiously again. For many years this has been a valuable way for me to work, and I have done so with a great variety of people.

One of the results is that the walls between me and others have steadily come down. It has become possible for me to feel love for any person I turn my attention to rather than only towards a few individuals or a type of person my patterns are attracted to. I used to think it was 'normal' to feel numb or indifferent about the majority of people. The discovery that I have the ability to see past people's patterns and feel love deeply for everybody has had great implications. My ability to be a powerful counsellor for others has dramatically increased. My feelings of emotional and sexual desperation have significantly decreased along with old addictive behaviours. I am enjoying making friends! There is a world full of people to be close to, and none of the separations caused by sexism, racism, ageism and so on need to be a barrier. I have developed long-term close friendships with people from backgrounds very different from my own. My picture of the world has expanded and my understanding of a diversity of groups in the population has deepened. Life has become fun and less of a struggle!

Eventually it occurred to me that if I could see so much goodness in others, logically I must have that same goodness. It had always been difficult for me to feel pleased with myself, but now I began to have glimpses of this and started to do more work in that direction. Occasionally the chronic humiliation that I and my family had carried all our lives would shift and I could more easily see that we had been wronged through no fault of our own. Finally I could feel my anger and begin to recover more fully my ability to fight for myself.

For several years I had been in a working-class support group in my RC Community where we had worked consistently on reclaiming pride in our people. I realised that I had 'escaped' to another city because of the harshness of the oppression and not because of any lack of caring or commitment to my people. I had also been programmed to get an education, leave the working class, and become middle class. Through many sessions, I decided this was not what I wanted and not who I was. After getting a good education, I left school, moved back to the neighbourhood I grew up in, got a job working as a machinist, and began organising. Although there have been many struggles, the profound connections I've been able to make with working-class people have been worth it, and my life has been transformed once again. I began teaching my friends Co-Counselling and we now have our own RC Community. These relationships have endured and flourished over decades now. They have also become a powerful source of leadership in the world as our influence has spread.

The RC Community is where I began to recover my visibility as an Arab. I remember a workshop in 1976, walking to a meeting with my first RC teacher, and telling her for the first time that I was Lebanese. She was not only aware of who Lebanese people are but also delighted to learn that it is part of my background. It was the most positive response I had received up to that point. RC has been a place where I have been able to meet Arabs, other people of colour, and our allies in a context of mutual support in recovering from the effects of racism while we work for its elimination. After growing up in a culture that in effect forced me and my family to be 'white', I have been able to reclaim my pride as an Arab man and reach more deeply towards my humanity and connection to the world.

As a man, I've found it possible to be fully human and caring with whomever I choose, rather than conforming to the narrow range of what a man is supposed to be and following society's dictates about who I can be close to. The realisation that intimacy need not be sexual gives me the opportunity of knowing an ocean of people in a meaningful way.

As a Catholic I've been able to find the wisdom in my family's traditional beliefs and live it to the best of my ability, while recovering my flexibility in how I understand and practise it. The Co-Counselling process has clarified that it is not necessary to reject the good in our cultural traditions or accept their rigidities uncritically. It is only the distress patterns passed on for generations that need to be discharged as we recover our ability to think freshly about these ancient ideas.

My health has benefited from persistent use of Re-evaluation Counselling. Besides physical activity and good nutrition, regular discharge seems to be a key component. Last month during a physical, my doctor, thinking I was much younger, looked startled when I told him my age. He asked, 'What have you been doing?' My optometrist notices that my prescription hasn't changed for many years and says things like, 'You must be eating your carrots' or 'Your eyes must be well rested.' With a family history of high blood pressure and 'trouble with our nerves', in many cases resulting in decades of dependence on medication, I use no medications and do not have high blood pressure.

Co-Counselling has truly been a life-saver. Although I still have distress patterns and know that full recovery will take more work, I have a good map of what the remaining hurts are and where I need to persist with discharge. I have a long-term perspective of my progress over time, even through periods when I had difficulty seeing forward movement. Perhaps the most noticeable change is how much I enjoy life and am at peace with it. The future looks good.

New to parenting: Sarah's and Helen's stories

Sarah and Helen are white Englishwomen who Co-Counsel with each other regularly and have started a mothers' support group. Sarah is now 27 and Helen 30, and they have been Co-Counselling since they were teenagers. They both have baby sons.

Sarah comes from a working-class family. Helen is middle class. Both are currently dependent on their partners' incomes. Helen said about this:

> Yes, it is an issue for me. It changes the dynamics of our relationship. But I still decided there was nothing more important I could be doing and that Finlay needed me on an everyday basis.

Sarah said:

> Yes, it is hard. Ed's really good about it, he never questions me, but if you've got your own money you feel independent. You've got power and status. If you haven't got these things, what you're doing usually isn't recognised as worth anything. But I don't want to go back to work till Jacob's at school or maybe at nursery school.

Sarah and Helen interviewed each other about how they've used Co-Counselling as mothers.

Helen: Tell me how you used Re-evaluation Counselling, Sarah, while you were pregnant and when Jacob was born.

Sarah: When I was at first pregnant with Jacob it was hard to feel pleased with myself. I remember feelings about being wrong, not being ready. I remember that first support group you organised. You and I had an arrangement that whoever got pregnant first, the other one would organise a support group – do you remember that? (*both laugh*). That was the deal.

I remember that in the first support group meeting I was feeling ashamed. It was hard to take in that everyone was there for me and that they were pleased with me. I had a huge cry trying to be pleased with myself as a mother. It took a long time for me to come to terms with being a mother, and me being OK. Those support groups every month made a big difference to me keeping on track and feeling good about myself, and basically just feeling all the feelings that came along.

I remember a big session I had with P. I was feeling resentful toward my unborn baby about all the attention he was getting, and all the attention that I didn't get. I had a huge cry about this. After that, it was much easier for me to feel my full love for my baby. I remember P talking about pain because I was scared about giving birth. She said that pain is just pain, that's all it is, and that you can feel it. I decided from then not to have any drugs at birth, since they could affect the baby.

I thought a lot about how I wanted it to be when Jacob was born. Co-Counselling made a big difference to the way I arranged it. I wanted a lot of people to be there, because I think a lot of people should be there when a person comes into the world.

Helen: Who was with you?

Sarah: I had my mum, my sister, my auntie, Ed's mum and Ed of course, and a midwife as well. They were the people I most wanted Jacob to have a relationship with, right from the start. At one point during the labour it was getting hard. I wanted to do whatever it took to get him out, and the medical staff wanted to break my waters. I'd given my mum the role of making sure we held to my birth plan, where I wanted no interference, no drugs. The staff were trying to encourage me to let them break my waters, saying it would get things moving, and my mum stopped that from happening. I was in so much pain and so fed up, saying, 'When is it going to end?' and my mum said to me, 'It will end when it ends.' At that point I made a decision. I thought 'Yes! I can do it. It *will* end at some point.' Then it was quick; it was over in an hour to two hours after that. So that was a critical part – oooh – (*trembles and laughs*). I remember crying a lot round about his birth. I don't remember exactly how I was feeling, just that I was having huge cries, and that it was OK to cry. It was also important to me that Jacob was crying and that I knew it was OK for *him* to cry. I could just hold him and let him cry.

During those first three months it was difficult not knowing why he was crying and getting too caught up in thinking he might need feeding or whatever it was. I found it hard to know whether he needed to cry or he needed feeding, but I know there were times where he was able to cry and it was clear that he needed to.

Helen: What else do you remember?

Sarah: I've felt lonely, overtired, and overworked and that I cannot do this any more. I've felt absolutely terrible about myself, and it's felt like the truth about me, but I've known it was OK to cry. This made a huge difference – crying and crying and then not feeling so bad, knowing I'm not bad and that being a young mother is a hard set-up and a struggle.

Helen: What's been happy? (*laughs*)

Sarah: Just being able to have that joy. I don't know how many people get to have that. There are days when I realise what a joy it is, when I feel relaxed and easy and happy for Jacob to do whatever he wants. Those days make it all worthwhile.

Helen: How would you say you are different from most mums you know?

Sarah: My thinking is to treat Jacob as a *person*, with as much respect as I can. That means listening to what he has to say – when he talks, when he makes any kind of babbly noise, when he gestures for what he wants, when he wants to go places, when he wants to grab things, when he wants to look at things. All these things that he wants to do are important – what he wants to do is part of what makes him who he is. As a mother, I get to allow him to do all those things, to encourage him, to marvel at what he wants to do, to basically to pay attention to it. We don't have a set routine. We don't do the same things every day. Sometimes I feel useless because of that, but I think it's important to be flexible (*shakes, laughs*). I understand why people have routines – there is so much to do and so little time to do it in, but my priority is Jacob getting to do what he wants to do and to spend time with him.

I want him to get a sense of the world and of who he is. That's the most important thing for me. It used to feel like the most important thing was for the house to be clean and the food made. That's where RC made a huge difference. The most important thing is *him*.

How has Co-Counselling made a difference to you, Helen?

Helen: I had a support group which met every six weeks, and I got attention for how I was doing being pregnant. It helped me think about some of the big issues about being pregnant and being a mother, about my fears and hopes.

During the birth, Co-Counselling meant I knew it was fine to make a lot of noise and express myself, to do whatever I needed to do. I had some sessions on the phone while I was in the early stages of labour, and it was good not to feel alone with it. I was scared during the birth and hadn't anticipated that. Directly afterward, I was able to cry about what it had been like. I have more crying to do about that. I think getting over pain and fear from giving birth is important and sets a good tone for your relationship with your child.

Co-Counselling has made a difference on a practical level. I can tell people what it's actually like being a mum and don't have to pretend it's easy. In the early days I asked people to come in and listen to me, and I could tell them it was hard without thinking this meant there was something wrong with me or I was at fault for having these feelings.

I notice a way I'm different from other people in how I want to be with Finlay. I don't think I'm better than other parents; I can see they love their children. But sometimes they don't understand why I treat Finlay as I do. It looks to them like I'm indulging him. And sometimes it's difficult for me to watch how other people treat their children. I'm working in sessions on the fact that I do have lots in common with other parents.

I view babies as complete human beings who are aware of what's going on around them, who are hurt if they get ignored. I want to use Co-Counselling in such a way that Finlay will always have a sense of himself. When there are things wrong in the world or with people around him, I want him to be clear that *he's* all right. When he has feelings – if he feels sad or angry or whatever – I want him to be listened to so he can move on from those feelings rather than having to get stuck there.

He does lots of crying whenever I or my partner leave him. Don has had to work a lot and hasn't been with Finlay as much as I have. I think Finlay has been upset about this. When I have to go somewhere and he has to be with Don, Finlay at first acts like Don is the worst, worst person to be with, and he cries a lot. Then when I come back, he and Don are the best of friends, and he's relaxed and confident that his dad loves him as well as his mum.

Every day, for some period of time, I try to follow my son's lead. He likes to explore everything in the house in utter detail, repeatedly, looking in cupboards, exploring things outside, going inside and out, inside and out, and I let him do what he wants and not be shaped by me. When he wants to do things that are dangerous, I just say no and give him a chance to be upset. If something is too hot we wait till it's cooled down, or I hold it while he looks, or we do something else or go somewhere else.

He sleeps in our bed. I think that's important. It sometimes complicates my relationship with Don, but we've decided to do it.

Sarah: What else do you use Co-Counselling for?

Helen: Just staying sane. When I'm feeling especially bad, or when I'm being blamed, I can be clear that these are just my feelings or someone else's feelings, and that really I'm OK and they're OK (*laughs*). It's important as parents to talk about our feelings. Children have feelings, and they haven't learnt yet to not have them or to put them away. Parents get confused about feelings. They think, 'Why is my baby crying?' and feel bad about themselves and bad for the baby. If they just knew it was all right for the baby to cry, that he was crying about a difficult birth or whatever, their lives could be so much better.

Angela's story: getting my life back

Angela: I've been active in Re-evaluation Counselling for six and a half years. When I started Co-Counselling I claimed it as my own from the beginning. I immediately recognised it as something that would make a big difference in my life. Discharge made complete sense to me. I had been discharging – especially crying – all my life, although mostly not with people. I would set up situations where I could cry – listening to music, sitting in a tree and so on. I cried in isolation, but using the discharge process was not at all unfamiliar.

Katie: What was your first reaction to RC's assumptions about basic human nature and the goodness of reality?

Angela: It made complete sense to me. I grew up in an abusive situation, but I remember that at a particular point I realised I was independent of what was happening to me. I was able to hold on to something that made me less vulnerable to believing everything other people told me. I developed my own set of thoughts about how things are and should be, and I think that included what human beings are like inherently.

My dad and his partner had bought a 116-acre piece of property when I was 5 years old, and I felt connected to the trees and animals there. It gave me a place to relate to life that was outside of anything damaging to me. I could tell I was loved by some teachers and friends of the family, but I couldn't be myself around other people because of how I'd been hurt. I was too scared to show how hard my life was. But inside I did have that space to be myself, to feel free, and to dream and think about myself and life and the world in an unlimited way.

Katie: What were some of your early impressions of RC?

Angela: In my first Fundamentals class my teacher didn't pretend she 'had it all together', that she was the 'be-all and end-all'. She was herself. Sometimes she openly struggled through the class. There was something so human about her interactions with us. We all cuddled up while sitting close to each other. We followed her leadership and we were peers at the same time.

The most significant thing about me and Co-Counselling is my recovery from the devastation of the first sixteen years of my life. I was abused during these years and left with a particularly heavy chronic feeling that permeated everything and made living life hard. I had to come up against that heavy feeling every day to accomplish anything. And I got over it by discharging. The whole atmosphere of my life changed.

I'm African American. My sister and I were raised by my dad, who is African American, and because of the ways racism affected him, our lives were difficult. He had a hard time, and the effects of that filtered down to me and my sister. I was abused, excluded from my family, and told I was worthless. These experiences created an environment of misery in my mind that was incredibly pervasive.

Over the years I became more and more hopeless about any chance for help. I was unable to see outside of the distorted picture I'd been shown. Because I had been frightened by my experiences, I became scared to relate to anybody on my own terms. As a young adult I remember thinking that some people just aren't happy, that happiness is a myth. The misery was all pervasive; I felt it was just the way things were. I had few opportunities to have close contact with people because I was too scared to take up space. I couldn't say what I thought or take any risks. I did not feel entitled to have the life I wanted, especially if it would inconvenience anyone else – and that is also part and parcel of racism, which got laid in on top of those early experiences. I can't describe how miserable I've been.

So for me, Co-Counselling was about feeling better. (I envied some other Co-Counsellors, who seemed able to dip in and out of feelings on their way to regaining their thinking and full selves.) It was also about saving my life. I couldn't actually live my life if I didn't feel better. I couldn't drag myself out of bed. Lifting a finger was like moving through molasses. It was like throwing myself up against this wall, over and over again, to do something as simple as wash the dishes or take on anything I really wanted to do.

All the accomplishments in my life have been achieved through this heavy veil of intense feelings. It was so frustrating because I have always had a sense of who I am. I have a mind that can think in far-reaching ways – for example, about what's wrong in the world and how to change it. It was incredibly painful to wake up and be able to think (cries) but to only be able to get as far as getting myself out of bed, getting dressed and brushing my teeth – and thinking maybe I'd floss my teeth but knowing doing it was not likely (laughs). But that's what I could do, without making tremendous additional efforts – which I did make to keep functioning. To have so many years of not being able to reach what I knew I could do (cries) was incredibly painful and also incredibly discouraging. Because of this, on top of the hurt from abuse was a feeling of failure – I felt like I was constantly failing because I could not come close to reaching what I wanted to do and what I knew was possible.

The way my life was going in my late twenties, it seemed my ability to function was diminishing, and so I did less and less. I had increasingly less of myself available to me.

When I started Co-Counselling I didn't know if it was possible to get through that whole set of feelings, but I knew Co-Counselling would be immensely helpful. I knew intuitively that this was the thing for me, and I took it on that way. I cried as much as I could with as many people as I could. I used every form of it intensely. Because I was working part-time, I could put a lot of time and effort into it.

An important thing is that I've never acted 'crazy'. None of my friends had any clue that what I've described has been my experience in life. I functioned. I went to work. I went to school and got good grades. Nobody knew I had this huge struggle, that this was what it was like to live my life.

If I had gone to a psychiatrist I probably would have been prescribed drugs. I specifically decided not to seek therapy because I was sure someone would label me manic-depressive. I could see that nobody was going to be able to understand me as well as I understood myself. It seemed clear that if I didn't stay in charge, I was going to be lost. Only I could unravel my despair. I hadn't thought it through this clearly at that time, but it makes sense – that if somebody had gotten in there and mucked around and tried to 'fix' me, I would have been lost. I'd been mucked around with my whole life – my difficulties were from people having messed with me. I wouldn't be able to undo the damage by adding more of the same.

Co-Counselling also gave me a place to reach beyond where I felt I could do things. There was encouragement to take leadership. For me, this was an incredible contradiction to the places where I felt like I couldn't do anything. Trying to lead pushed me up against the feelings of 'I can't do it', and gave me the opportunity to discharge those feelings.

About a year ago I was feeling worse and worse and was having thoughts of suicide. I never thought I was going to commit suicide, except for one scary time. But it felt like things were getting harder. At the same time I could tell that the process was working. Things were getting better. There were times when I was happy. There were times when I could feel an absence of the heavy feelings; then they would return, and I would again feel sunk and stuck. So I did have these glimpses, and they gave me something to hold on to. I could tell that things were moving.

Apparently my progress had given me a strong enough foundation that I could feel the worst of my feelings. There came a period of time during which I felt worse than I had ever felt. I felt so bad I couldn't tell that I wouldn't kill myself. It wasn't that I wanted to end my life; it was that my mind was searching for any way out of this misery, and it would keep going to suicide as an option. It seemed the only option I could find and I couldn't tell that I wouldn't do it. I realised it was me, or those feelings.

At this point I decided to set up a large number of sessions so that I could work intensively on the core feelings that I now had access to. It felt like an effort to save my life. I was strategic in choosing my counsellors for this intense effort. They knew me well and had a good picture of my struggles. Some of them weren't the most experienced Co-Counsellors, but they knew how to let me know they were on my side, and I knew they would not get in my way but would back me in what I was trying to do.

A certain amount of risk-taking had already happened in these Co-Counselling relationships. We'd been able to discharge with each other on difficult areas – such as about sex or sexual abuse. We'd gotten through times of attaching old feelings to each other – we'd discharged them, keeping the Co-Counselling relationship clean as a Co-Counselling relationship. Sometimes the risk-taking had simply been that somebody had made a mistake and I had fought my way through to have that mistake corrected. I had cried about how it felt, and the other person had cried about being sorry about it and had apologised, and we had ended up closer than we were before the mistake had been made. When you get to that point with somebody, you become closer. So my close relationships with my counsellors were important in making my counselling go well.

I was strategic about attacking this distress. I already had a good picture of it from all the discharging I'd done previously. I knew where I needed to put my mind in order to discharge the core feelings. I worked and discharged with the intention of ending the miserable feelings forever. I started out talking and discharging on that topic. I would cry and cry and cry, or get mad.

The counsellors took my lead. I presented as clear a picture as I could of what the distress was and where I thought I needed to go, and the counsellors would counsel me there and keep holding up to me what I had told them. I would keep discharging there. Then I would offer more information from my perspective, and so on. After a few days I was doing a lot of re-evaluating. All sorts of new thoughts and perspectives came spontaneously. My picture of myself in the world began to change dramatically. I was arriving at a completely different perspective about my life.

As a result of this intense period of counselling, the hugely uncomfortable feelings were mostly discharged. Over the next period of time things kept sifting and filtering through my mind as I continued to re-evaluate.

About seven months later, I took a week-long trip. When I came back home, *everything* was different! Apparently I had just needed a break from the usual restimulation of my everyday life to realise all the gains I'd made. I'd gotten a break, was around different people doing different things, and I came back and everything was different! And it's been that way ever since! I have not had the pervasive feeling of misery that had almost always been with me. I've had hard times and some miserable days, but I haven't been in molasses at all, not once since then (*laughs*). I mean, it's been a permanent shift!

I now have an incredible amount of access to my life. I have an amazing number of choices. I've made new friends. I've gotten more politically active. I read the newspaper. I mean, I've never been able to read the newspaper – and I'd beat myself up about it: 'You just need to read the newspaper!' But, 'Oh, it's too depressing, it's too something.' But it was really that I didn't have the space or attention for it in my mind. But now I *can* read the newspaper! I can read two newspapers in a day if I want to! (*laughs*)

And I take more risks. I'm working on a big project. It's been upsetting at times because I feel like I'm way out ahead of where I have ever been before, but I'm able to do it. I've occasionally gotten in trouble. People have gotten mad at me. This is because I'm not so careful anymore. I used to have to be sure that I only took on what I could handle. I had to control the restimulation that might come up. So I always made sure that everybody was OK, that I wouldn't get myself into a situation I couldn't get out of, because doing that seemed likely to end my life – I could not handle one more bit of bad feelings than I already had to deal with. And that's gone! I really have access to my life. I'm going to school in the fall; I'm going to get my college degree, which I've wanted to do every year – but each year couldn't remember in time to apply to college! (*laughs*)

I'll tell one way my perspective has changed. My former perspective, even though I was an adult, was that I was still little. I functioned in the world as if I was still little. After discharging the core hurt, the world was still essentially the same, but what was different was that I now realised I wasn't little. That I was BIG. This change of perspective meant that everything I now came in contact with, whether it was another human being, a car, a tree, was seen in a different light. I was re-evaluating my relationship to everything in the world based on my new perspective. It had far-reaching implications. For one thing, I know I am in charge of my life. This is a completely new basis for my mode of operation.

I'll talk about the part racism played in all this. My early hurts made me especially vulnerable to believing the negative messages that came at me from society about myself as a black woman, messages such as 'I'm stupid', 'I'm not worth anything'. 'Everybody else in the world gets to have their way, but I have to sacrifice myself, my opinions, my ideas, my voice, and yield to everybody else, to other people of colour and to white people.' Changing my perspective has given me a leg up on that piece of distress. I'm big! Things don't scare me in the same way as they did before.

I remember that during this period of intense counselling, I went to the local drug store and was followed in the store. Because of racism, this is not an unusual experience for black people. A woman passed me, then came back to watch me, then came and stood next to me, and then followed me. It felt devastating. It was good that I had a lot of sessions set up, because I had a place to go to sift through the experience. In my sessions I used the phrase, 'I'm queen of the world' as a way to get a picture of myself outside the feelings of victimisation. As I cried and laughed taking this perspective, I came up with responses such as, 'Can I help *you?*' (*laughs*) 'Could somebody else please help her; I've got better things to do' (*laughs*). I unhooked from feeling devastated by that event. My mind became free to put it in perspective, to realise that what happened actually had nothing to do with me.

I'll talk some about racism, oppression, building community, and the role of taking on the distresses of the world (*laughs*). I'm actually writing an article about this right now.

One of the things that happens to particular constituencies of people is that we get separated from each other because of the hurts that happened to us. It is so painful to have this negative stuff aimed at us that we aim it at each other. We direct it at each other, and it gets in our way of having each other. One incredible thing that Co-Counselling has given me is the ability to reach for black people and have them as never before – not only in Co-Counselling but outside of Co-Counselling as well. My relationships with black people are much better and much clearer than they have ever been in my life. I can tell that I want my people in a way that's soft and open. There's something about being with a group of people who share a set of distresses that have been laid in by society, that's an incredible break from the isolation of feeling like my struggles are just my own, that they're my fault. I not only get to see people with similar-looking struggles, but I get to see them fight their way through. I'm not an isolated individual with something wrong with me, but just one of the many who have been hurt and are working our way out of it.

The one-point programme of RC is to reclaim our full intelligence and help others to do the same. As an African American person, I used to feel, 'Well, that's really letting a lot of people off the hook! A lot of people are being hurt by oppression, and all that RCers are expected to do is have sessions and discharge whatever they want to discharge!' I don't see it that way anymore. I think the one-point programme is right; I just have a less limited perspective on it. I've defined full intelligence and what it means to really reclaim it, more broadly. Now I take the one-point programme to include *making sure that the world reflects intelligence and not distress*. It seems to me that many RCers take it this way as well.

Sylvia's story: success in a long struggle with violence patterns

Sylvia: When, in 1974, at the age of 29, I joined my first Re-evaluation Counselling class, I didn't realise I was being introduced to a body of ideas, a process and a community of fellow human beings that would help me eliminate a violence pattern that had haunted me and influenced my life from early childhood. For most of my life I had daydreamed of 'going crazy' and killing people because I thought it would be fun and exciting. In fact, in 1968, at the age of 23, one year after my father had died, fantasy had become reality and I had made a down-payment on a revolver and purchased an enormous hunting knife with the hope of fulfilling this longing to kill people.

Since it's a long story, I will summarise: two psychiatric hospitalisations totalling nine months, one suicide attempt, medications and twelve electro-convulsive therapy (ECT) treatments later, I ended up back in the community. I was both mystified and frightened by my behaviour and convinced that I would never lead a 'normal' life. Despite this pessimism, I assumed I had been 'helped'. Little did I know. Because of the largely ineffective nature of conventional therapies, the pattern lay dormant (of course) and, like any pattern, needed only the right elements for re-activation. Fortunately, I had begun Co-Counselling, and whenever this specific collection of elements appeared, I was ready for the pattern with the discharge process and the Co-Counselling relationships I had set up. My experience shows that this kind of pattern, like all patterns, can melt away when confronted by loving, patient human beings who help the person wield the discharge process.

Yes, the melting process took a while, but it was such a special while. First, there was the gradual realisation that my daily interactions with people at my workplace were becoming easier and therefore more rewarding. Then there was learning to feel and enjoy affection and closeness (goodbye isolation – you fooled me into thinking solitariness was fun, but I've cracked your cowardly code). There was laughter, tears and raging. And there was question and discovery. All became clear. Everyone's goodness was revealed, and I got to be my human self, without pretence.

I'm sure I'm not the only RCer who has worked on dismantling the patterns and sub-patterns that allow one to believe that homicide would be 'fun' or 'fulfilling'.

Pivotal counselling sessions

The first direction I used was urged upon me in 1974 by my first Co-Counsellor (I remember who you are!) in my first out-of-class session. Because of her persistence, I unlocked an entire set of distress patterns in one session. The direction was, 'I am, and always was, a good person'. My counsellor persisted in urging me to repeat it in a variety of ways (different tones, volumes, pitches and so on) until, to my astonishment, I burst into heavy sobbing. When I finished sobbing, I said, 'I didn't think I *was* good'. I then sobbed some more. We repeated this sequence until all discharge ceased. After that session, in spite of whatever was going on in my life, I never again doubted my goodness. My first Co-Counsellor gave me a priceless gift – one I still use today, every day.

In 1979 I discharged for the first time some of the rage I had felt as an infant and child. By doing so, I reduced the likelihood that ordinary life stresses would trigger the 'wouldn't it be fun to go crazy and kill people' pattern. This discharge was possible because my Co-Counsellor and teacher, C, had grinned broadly and delightedly at me when I was seized by a desire to say to him, 'I'm so frustrated by problems with my memory that I could kill.' His expression of delight allowed me to dare to put attention on this statement and pursue a chain of thoughts. The following is taken from my session notes: 'I could kill.' (C grins broadly and delightedly at me. I let more feelings surface.) 'I could kill *you*.' I sob and laugh. '*I could kill you!*' I scream. (C says, 'Keep saying that, Sylvia.') 'I want to kill you!' (C nods and smiles lovingly.) 'I want to kill you!' Sob. 'I want to kill . . . ' I scream from the bottom of my toes. 'I know who I want to kill.' Laugh. Cry. (C: 'I bet you do.') I scream, cry and laugh. 'I wanted to kill my father.' Scream. This session was a turning point.

In a session in the late 1980s I was saying, 'I want to kill . . . ' and the words that came out were: ' . . . *both* my parents'. Sobbing and roaring followed. This was a shocking realisation. I had thought, as a result of the 1979 session, that I had wanted to kill only my father. When I stopped discharging, I said to B, with amazement, 'I don't think I'll ever want to kill anyone again. Now I know I wanted to kill *both* of *them*. So killing just any people would *never* bring any satisfaction.' I felt disappointment. I had a long way to go before I gained access to memories of incidents that installed the pattern, and a long way before I fully understood my parents' personal hurts and their prodigious efforts to be the good and loving human beings they were. Nevertheless, because of the discharge process, in this particular session the pattern lost its power to generate any prolonged emotion or desire. It was, in essence, dead.

RC, reassuring and effective

Throughout the years I've been reassured by all of RC's assumptions, but two things kept me away from hospital emergency rooms and were life-saving: (1) the assumption of our inherent goodness, and (2) the natural healing process. These two helped me avoid panic! When I was caught in a patterned fantasy, I was able to remind myself that I was a good human being who was being restimulated by some elements in my situation and I simply needed to discharge. I was not a bad person who was falling apart.

Thanks to RC theory, I had a valuable guide for recognising another distress pattern: of liking, loving and being intrigued by what I feared and what upset me. I 'loved' weapons and wanted to own and use them because, when I was small, I had been threatened with them and they frightened me. I 'loved' and therefore sought out and bonded with authoritarian teachers (whether or not they were effective teachers) because they reminded me of my mother when she was distressed, and this frightened me. I 'loved' driving at seventy miles per hour when surrounded by tractor-trailer trucks because I feared for my life. This love-what-you-fear-or-what-upsets-you pattern was life-threatening because it prevented me from grasping the reality of harmful or dangerous situations.

We have a role to play

We in RC have a role to play in helping our fellow human beings who have been inflicted with violence patterns. I think about my US culture and its institutionalised violence patterns. I think about victims of violence who unwittingly rehearse their own distress on a nationwide scale by writing, producing, and marketing violent movies and television shows. These dramatic rehearsals, no matter how entertaining they seem to be, replace healing with restimulation, and they reactivate isolation patterns. When I think of these things, I know I'm not going to settle for anything less than completely good lives for my fellow survivors of violence patterns.

This article is the first step on a new RC quest. It is also an opportunity to publicly thank all the people with whom I have Co-Counselled over the years. Thank you.

Sylvia

Letters to and from Harvey

These are excerpts from correspondence between Harvey Jackins and Sylvia over a period of thirty years. They explain how the article above came to be written.

December 19 1978

Dear Sylvia,

Many thanks for your letter of December 10. Your letter on your progress was very good. I think something like this would be excellent for *Recovery and Re-emergence* [the RC journal for 'mental health' system survivors]. It would mean a lot to many people. I think the story of somebody fighting out of that deep distress to good functioning would be quite inspiring for everyone in the field.
With love,
Harvey

December 26 1978

Dear Harvey,

Many thanks for your letter. I will definitely write an article for *Recovery and Re-emergence*. I can concisely describe a number of instances in which RC saved me from getting lost in what we would call distress patterns and what professionals might call symptoms of regression, delusions. (Only one, thank heaven, has ever appeared – the fear that I might be Jesus reincarnated. Thanks to RC, I was only afraid I might be, never confident that I *was*, Jesus.)

Anyway, my initial diagnosis in 1968 was: schizophrenic reaction, undifferentiated type, acute and chronic, with psychotic depression. Labels are only labels, and who knows if every professional would have made such a diagnosis. But I do know I was pretty far off base all my life. You (and I) can understand why for four years I have told myself, and others, that RC (and my roommate who learned to counsel me RC-fashion) has saved my life. My gratitude to my Co-Counsellors has always been intense, though not always expressed. When I learned the diagnosis recently, some feelings and patterns surfaced, but they didn't throw me. Thanks to our theory my reactions were new routes to discharging distress. I have been terribly lucky.

Best of luck in the next round of workshops. Feel free to mention my experience and me anytime. I'm not hiding. My hope is that once I'm free of my particular distress patterns, I will then stand up and declare, 'We can recover from anything'.

With love and confidence,

Sylvia

April 4 1979

Dear Sylvia,

Thanks for your dear letter. I am delighted that your 'hysteria', silliness, and laughter are spilling out. All is indeed well. 'Blossom by blossom the spring begins.'

With love,

Harvey

May 25 1979

Dear Harvey,

I just have to tell you that I'm still making encouraging progress. I'll try to be concise because I can imagine how busy you are.

Through using RC, I have re-discovered how painful and frightening my childhood was. I seriously believed my father wanted to kill me (reasons as yet unknown why I felt this way). At some point as a child I definitely wanted to kill him. This desire was eventually translated into 'I want to kill someone' and was expressed in fantasies, from at least grade four on, in which I was a boy who was a criminal or maniac. I never realised until a session just this Wednesday that I switched my identity in order to cope with the powerful desires to kill 'someone'. I finally felt a little of that on Wednesday – not as anger, but as grief that I couldn't kill someone, hadn't killed someone, had lost my chance to kill someone. While I was feeling that grief, I realised that as a child I suspended my ability to feel anger because to me anger meant killing someone. It also was clear to me that I feel afraid to release anger in Co-Counselling because of the fear that I will go into a rage I can't control. (I know that in time, when there is enough safety, I will release it. I also suspect there was a definite event when I was a child during which I had to be restrained when a child – either because I was angry and was being prevented from expressing it, or because I was in a victim position and was being physically abused.) Anyway, I'm closer. Many of my patterns are 'up', but I'm using them to get to the real feelings. Also, lately I've experienced some fear in my dreams. I'm glad.

I spoke publicly last night, and before and afterward I let my body release fear by permitting myself to tremble and my teeth to chatter. Probably not noticeable to the audience. Anyway, I spoke clearly. Did well. I will always let myself discharge when I am afraid. It's my earned privilege to feel fear and to discharge.

Harvey, take good care. Don't answer this letter. You have enough to do.
Love,
Me (Sylvia)

May 31 1979

Dear Sylvia,

Thanks for your note of May 25. I am glad things continue to come out and make sense. I'm sure there is an occluded incident with lots of violent 'killing' language in it that will eventually surface, but I don't want you to bring it up until it comes up by itself.

I am so pleased with you.
With much love,
Harvey

October 24 1979

Dear Harvey,

It's time to tell you that, thanks to RC, I continue to make progress as far as my recovery of myself goes. The following patterns no longer 'work' (neither elevate my mood nor distract me): eating, daydreaming about going crazy, thinking about guns and knives, remembering past homicidal fantasies, and reading my medical report and its diagnosis. I get no feelings of excitement or stimulation from them. (Actually, sometimes I get a second's feeling of excitement, or, I find myself trying the patterns out with a mild longing that they would 'work'.)

Another change that dismayed me at first and that I have somewhat come to terms with involves a reduction in my desire to involve myself in others' problems. My save-everyone yearnings have been converted to 'if you're in a crisis and need a tremendous amount of time and attention and love, don't ask me for it; right now I don't *want* to give it'. I still don't know what to think of this development; you can imagine some of the thoughts and questions I have.

Most of the above developments have occurred since I moved to this city to live alone. Since the move, in sequence, the following has occurred: feeling kind of funny, especially mornings; finally identifying it as loneliness and about the same time noticing that in the morning it was especially easy to wonder if life was worth living, if I was worth living; becoming extra sensitive to the hurts in the world, especially others'; and wondering if existing was worth all the pain. I felt like life was not worth the pain, that there was no purpose in existence outside of the purposes we invented ourselves – and I wondered how I could invent my own when life wasn't worth the pain anyway. Realising that without my patterns there would be no 'breaks'; I was stuck here in this body until I died (this thought brought real terror). Wondering if I ought to give up my 'selfish' goal of taking a biology course, give myself to God, and using His strength spend my life saving my friends. Terror, emptiness, and grief just bubbled during the months of August and September.

Then – a crisis in September. I survived it and accepted the fact that life would mean constant interruptions of my goal-centered activities and that interruptions could be survived. I didn't have to abandon my goals. That was a real breakthrough.

So now, for the first time since August, I'm feeling relatively at peace with myself. I'm taking a college course in biology. I have no set life goal, no solid career plans, and I'm handling the uncertainty well. I expect future periods of turmoil as I resolve past hurts that prevent me from being happily homosexual or heterosexual. I think I am more in the real world than I have ever been. And I am the most real. Life is harder, human relationships are more complex, than I ever imagined. There's no euphoric state to convince me there is meaning and purpose in everything, and no manic energy to carry me out in the world saving my friends.

Off and on through this process, since 1974, I have thought, 'I didn't know life was like *this*'. Life without fantasies and automatic mood-changers certainly is different. It *feels* worse than I expected, but that's OK. For the first time I hold most of the reins. Now that I can see the terrain more clearly, I can engage in that lifelong process of course-setting and course-revision.

Harvey, I think of you a lot, especially when I'm thinking of how lucky I've been.

With love and thankfulness
Me (Sylvia)

October 31 1979

Dear Sylvia,

Many thanks for your letter of October 24, with the very real, sober estimate of where you are. It sounds good to me. What especially sounds good is that you are taking a course in biology and reaching for knowledge. It seems to me that what will finally engage your attention well, and permanently lift your spirits, is the enormous curiosity which all of us have to know more about the universe in which we exist. As you discard the patterns which you clung to for survival, I think you will take a deep satisfaction in knowing more about the world and doing more about it. Perhaps I'm only projecting my own attitude here, because curiosity and the delight of learning have kept me going for a long time. I do couple it with action, in part, perhaps, in a patterned way. I am delighted that you are giving up the patterned involvement in other people's troubles as you prepare to think through what you really want to do and start doing it.

It's very good to hear from you. I have enormous respect for you.
With love,
Harvey

Twenty years later

June 3 1999

Dear Harvey,

Sylvia here. I cherish images of you at the gathering in Connecticut.

Back in 1974, after I'd been in RC for awhile, I wrote to you thanking you for RC because it was helping me deal with my childhood and young adulthood pattern of wanting to kill people. This pattern had almost killed me when I was twenty-three (suicide attempt), and nearly allowed me to kill several other people, family included, before I was twenty-three. That twenty-third year I had been diagnosed schizophrenic, hospitalised, and given electric shock. When I began RC I was thirty, unaware that the pattern (and its various sub-patterns – 'violence is fun, being alone is exciting, to kill people would be fulfilling') was still influencing my life.

Anyway, that letter which I mailed you was printed, anonymously and with my permission, in *Present Time*.

RC has healed the pain and eliminated that pattern. And now, at fifty-four, I'm contemplating the number of young people trapped in such patterns and wondering if I'm ready to share what I have learned about eradicating homicide-related distress patterns. Because of RC I now know exactly what childhood experiences contributed to this obsession with murder. But, more important, I know how RC and its postulates, theory, and practices enabled me to ultimately dissolve the patterns.

I can say with great delight that I've used RC in peer counselling sessions probably forty-two weeks out of every year since 1974. This is why *I'm in one piece!*

Finally, let me say again as I often said in the past, *Thank you.*

With love,

Sylvia

June 4 1999

Dear Sylvia,

I do think it would make sense for you to prepare an article summarising your experience with your patterns and your successful outliving them. I would like to know what you would say, at least roughly, ahead of time. This is part of the *Guidelines* – if you put anything out that widely you are expected to check with the International Reference Person before it goes out. I'd be delighted to have you be a spokesperson for RC.

With much love,

Harvey

George's story: an important Co-Counselling relationship

George: I'm 53 years old. I live in the Midlands in Britain, where I was born. I was raised working-class, and grew up on a big council housing estate in Coventry. My father was an unskilled worker in the car industry. I'm the oldest of four children. While I was a young child my mother was a housewife who did occasional part-time cleaning jobs or other work. Later she worked as a community midwife. I went to an all-boys big comprehensive secondary school from the age of 11, and when I left school I went into the engineering industry as an apprentice.

Most of the jobs I've done have been connected with engineering. When my wife and I decided to have children, I left my job to be home with the children full-time. My wife is a teacher and she didn't want to stop work. Those were some of the best years of my life. I was at home for about eight years until my youngest daughter started school. I'd developed an interest in photography and I started looking for work as a community photographer and did that for about six years.

I knew a couple of people who were Co-Counsellors. This was about ten years ago. The overall effect of their interactions with me was to make me question a lot of assumptions I had had about the world. I eventually got into an RC fundamentals class which my friend taught.

The key thing that attracted me to RC was a simple idea. I'm a bit of a compulsive listener, but here was a situation where for every minute you put in, someone else was offering to listen to you for the same amount of time. And who listened to me in my life? Even now I find myself wondering why anyone would *want to* listen to me – that's the way my distress sits. I didn't have trouble talking when people did offer to listen. I didn't have much trouble crying about things. I used to cry before I did Co-Counselling, but always by myself. I used to hide it around other people.

I remember being impressed by the first workshops I attended. One workshop was held in a big old manor house that had been taken over by the trade union movement in the 1930s. They had raised a levy in the local district to buy it and to do it up. At the workshop, I had session after session thinking about the workmanship in the building, the craftsmanship in the gold leaf in the dining hall. I kept thinking, why weren't the names of the people who built the place up outside in big letters on the front of the building? All sorts of things about class came up for me, and I remember shaking like a leaf, which had never happened before.

My counselling relationship with Wendy has been the most significant one since I started Co-Counselling. It's been about six years now. For the last four years we've had Co-Counselling sessions regularly, even though for most of that time we've lived a two-hour drive away from each other. We counsel on the phone most days, albeit for just a short time.

It often feels to me that it's a real privilege to counsel people, that they would trust me and feel safe enough to share their struggles with me. If you do that enough with one person over time, something valuable builds up. One of the key things about my relationship with Wendy is that I am a working-class heterosexual man, and she doesn't share those identities. There's great value of someone being outside the groups you belong to and being able to offer a perspective you don't have. I think she'd say the same.

I value the different perspective Wendy's able to offer. She has encouraged me to pay attention to things I don't readily think of because of being working class. One of them is my health and physical well-being. Another one is my development as an artist. I would not have pursued art if it hadn't been for her constant encouragement. It was difficult in the early days to even consider identifying as an artist on any level. That's changed out of all recognition.

I think I'm a good counsellor for her because I can think in some areas where she struggles, and I am completely committed to her. Yesterday morning, for instance, I was driving to my parents' house to do a job for them, and she phoned me up because she was struggling. She's someone for whom I stop what I'm doing if she needs it. I just listened to her for half-an-hour. We didn't swap time on that occasion (it always evens out later). Because I know her well, having listened to her such a lot, I know what her key struggles are, so I'm able to give her a hand quite easily. But that's taken six years to build.

Caroline: What impact has this Co-Counselling relationship had on your life?

George: It would be a mistake to single one relationship out as the only influence, but I can think generally about how my life's different. One key thing would be my ability to be close to men. I remember at the beginning, when I was first Co-Counselling, it was a strange idea to hold hands with or hug other men. Over the course of time that's changed a lot. I've become relaxed about it.

I guess another key area is confidence in my ability to think – about anything, really. This is something Wendy has pushed. In the early days I was scared, terrified really, to share my thinking with people in almost any context. I've learnt that I *can* think about things, and I'm much more willing to risk sharing my thinking – like I'm doing right now (*laughs*). When I say share my thinking I mean sharing original thinking.

Wendy helped me get confidence in my thinking in several ways. She would listen to me, constantly encouraging me to think, and say things that suggested that there was something valuable about what went on in my head. She would push me, often to where I felt quite uncomfortable, to share my thoughts about almost anything. Besides talking, I did a lot of crying, shaking and laughing, but the aim was to go against my chronic pattern of believing that any thoughts that went on in my head were worthless.

A struggle we have with each other is to do with our class differences. I often find her owning-class patterns difficult. She encourages me to talk about that with her. I've also encouraged her to talk about what she can't stand about working-class behaviour, but it's difficult for her to accept that I might be able to listen to that. I think she works on that with other people, but when I have the chance, I encourage her to do this because my guess is she doesn't get enough opportunity. Sometimes I'll have sessions with other people about her patterns. A couple of times we've got a third Co-Counsellor in to help.

When I first started Co-Counselling I tried to use at home what I was learning in RC, but in a ham-fisted way. As I've gotten over this, my wife can more easily listen to me and let me know she appreciates Co-Counselling.

Flexible application of Co-Counselling

Both Wendy and I are leaders in our RC Community, so sometimes we've taken turns putting attention on things that happen in the Community, including thinking about the person who leads the Community.

I like the way the exchange of attention can be flexible. Something we've done is to take turns teaching each other things. We set aside an hour or so for one of us to teach the other something we thought it would be useful for him or her to know. Wendy still talks about two 'classes' I gave her (*laughs*). Bearing in mind that she's an owning-class woman, I wanted to get her to appreciate and grasp the significant contributions that working-class people make to the world. I chose to do that by asking her to sit down in front of the chair she often used when she worked in her studio, and I asked her how she thought that chair came to be. She began to think aloud about the different production processes that had been involved in its making. On some level she was already aware of many things that people sometimes might not realise. But she did not mention some things, including the raw materials, and I asked her to think about those things. The process of doing that was significant. She released a lot of feelings, and it led to a major re-evaluation for her to be confronted with that question.

The second 'class' happened because I'd spent some time myself in a café in a bus station, and I was noticing for my own benefit some things I respected about working-class people as they went about their everyday lives. When we later decided to do another 'class' for each other, I asked Wendy to go and sit in the café and open her eyes to what was going on. I didn't set the agenda; I left the learning to her. I had the idea that for her, and for many other people who don't move in that environment, there would be things they could learn there, as there were for me. What happened was that she took something quite different from the things that were going on in the café. She had been watching what was happening in the relationships between a number of people there. She said she learnt something about leadership and what it means to be a counsellor. There were a number of isolated groups of people, individuals and couples, in the café. There was a woman sitting in the centre, who was talking about a coach journey, and was appealing to these various people to give her attention. This isn't what we think of as Co-Counselling, but through her actions she was able to draw in those people and engage them in a way that looked useful to everybody, so that some sort of community developed. Wendy was impressed with that.

Once when Wendy was teaching me, she encouraged me to work on the idea of never again settling for anything less than everything. The effect of it was that I had to address the issue of my inherent power. I had a heavy session. I was shaking a lot. On the second occasion, Wendy decided it would be useful to have me look at my identity as a man. One question she asked was, 'What would it be like for me to give up the identity of being a man?' It was a way for me to become aware of hurtful conditioning that was part of that identity. I remember having a big session about that.

In these 'teaching' sessions, we were giving each other permission to direct the other person to places where they needed to learn something. By that time in our relationship we trusted each other's judgement enough to do that. These were important gifts we gave each other. To have a relationship like this makes a big difference.

Chapter 8

Re-evaluation Counselling in relation to other approaches

> 'Mental health' workers all, without exception, want to put an end to human suffering and to make things right and good for their clients and for all of humanity.
>
> (Re-evaluation Counseling 1991: 64)

In the early years of Re-evaluation Counselling, Harvey Jackins made contact with others in the field. His letter to a well-known psychiatrist was published as an RC pamphlet in 1970. A talk made to a county mental health association in California was published as 'The Art of Listening' (Jackins 1981b). An article on RC's relationship with other models appeared in the *Journal of Humanistic Psychology* (Somers 1972) and, in a companion article, the social implications of RC were discussed (Scheff 1972).

Harvey soon realised the extent of RC's divergence from other approaches and ended his investigations of them. He continued developing RC on its own terms, which included not mixing it with other theories and practices.

> Sometimes people are puzzled at our objections to their mixing other theories and practices with Re-evaluation Counseling because they have experienced or read about other therapists performing some actions very similar to some things the Re-evaluation Counselor does with his or her clients . . . the assumptions are different in the two cases, and this being so, the similarities can be ephemeral . . . To mix in other practices . . . is to saddle oneself with unfaced contradictions which can very quickly lead to harmful practices.
>
> (Jackins 1973a: 21–2)

The theory of Re-evaluation Counselling has successfully governed the practices of a number of professional counsellors and therapists who are also Co-Counsellors. RC reference persons for particular constituencies include one for mental health workers. Some of these professionals have published articles based on RC theory (for example, Bronstein 1984, 1986).

Situating RC

In attempting to situate RC among other approaches, we face a dilemma well expressed by Harvey Jackins:

> I have often been asked by members of lecture audiences to elucidate the differences between Re-evaluation Counseling and other approaches to human behavior . . . To attempt this requires that I, in a sense, describe these other systems to the audience, and this places me in a false position since I should not really speak for these other theories.
>
> (Jackins 1973a: 9)

We (the authors) have had little direct experience with other approaches. Our commentary on other models is based mostly on reading about them. We apologise in advance for any unintentional misrepresentations and encourage interested readers to seek information about these approaches from those informed by direct experience.

First, we will review the fundamental features of Re-evaluation Counselling – features which have been described more fully in earlier chapters of this book.

Eight key features of Re-evaluation Counselling

1 Our definition of intelligence, our description of the vulnerability of intelligence to interference by hurt, and the details of this interference are central to all that we do. The basis of human malfunction is interference with *intelligence* by hurtful experiences, *in very specific ways* (see Chapter 2).

2 We assume that the inherent nature of the human is integral, wholesome, profoundly intelligent, zestful, loving and good, and propose that *all* human beings have the capacity to flower and flourish far beyond what has so far been observed. The outstanding abilities which show up in some people are latent in everyone. Distress is a dysfunction rather than a 'bad side' of human beings.

3 We assume that *the only source of dysfunction* in a human being is an experience of hurt, either physical or emotional. Information taken in during that hurt experience is stored in the form of a rigid, compulsive pattern of feeling and behaviour rather than as usable information.

4 We recognise, and base our practice on, the *central importance* of the *full range of the discharge processes*. (The dependable outward indications of these processes are tears, trembling, perspiration, laughter, angry storming, non-repetitive talking and yawning.) When people have discharged sufficiently, they recover fully from the residual effects of distress experiences.

5 We have found that there is a distinct *difference between the inherent human being and the distress* that is parasitical upon him or her. This distinction influences RC practice in every aspect.

6   *The peer relationship is crucial in Re-evaluation Counselling.*
7   We recognise the *wider social context* as an important contributor to human hurt and have developed a practice to help people recover from socially imposed hurts.
8   We have found that it is helpful to be part of a group of people who share their collective resources of attention and increasing skill. The Re-evaluation Counselling Communities enhance individual re-emergence from distress.

These key features will be mentioned often as we compare RC with other approaches to human behaviour.

There are hundreds of approaches to counselling and psychotherapy (Palmer *et al.*1996; Stevens 1998). Among these are many different notions of recovery and good functioning. For the sake of simplicity, we will focus on selected versions of a few well-known approaches: biopsychiatry, psychoanalysis, behaviourism and humanistic psychology, and on only a few aspects of each. We also take the opportunity to discuss some points of RC theory which have not been brought out in earlier chapters of the book, and which distinguish RC from these approaches.

Biopsychiatry and the medical model

The medical model lumps together different ways of feeling, thinking and behaving and defines these as 'mental illness', which is viewed as a pathology with an organic base which should be treated by doctors. Even in countries with traditional ways of assisting distressed people, biopsychiatry now exists alongside the older methods and has higher status (Warner 1985).

In the mid-nineteenth century, doctors campaigned successfully to be recognised as experts in the care of the 'mad', though all they had to offer in the way of treatment was emetics, opiates, purges, cold baths, leeches and whirling machines. 'Moral management', a relatively successful non-medical approach (an ancestor of behavioural modification and occupational therapy), had been pioneered in some small private asylums (Digby 1985). Doctors secured legal backing for their claim that moral management should be used only under medical supervision. Since that period, 'madness' has increasingly been seen as an illness, and as the business of specialist doctors, that is, of psychiatrists. As in the nineteenth century, the present-day claim of psychiatry to dominance rests on social policy rather than clinical success. And, unfortunately, the multimillion-dollar pharmaceutical industry finances most psychiatric associations and research (Breggin 1993).

According to the medical model, organic problems are the basic cause of 'mental illness'. Even where psychological or environmental factors are admitted, these are assigned a secondary status (as 'stress' or 'triggers'). The patient's life experience and situation, including the effects of oppression, are not seen as key, since the problem is believed to be a distinct pathological condition of the brain.

When a psychiatrist has decided on a specific diagnosis, he or she will generally prescribe drugs. Since the coming of Community Care policies in the late twentieth century, in most countries people are no longer shut up in hospitals for years, but only for months or weeks. They are then discharged into the community, usually still on medication, where they continue to suffer the stigma of being a 'mental' patient. RC former 'mental patients' write: 'It has never been rational to label us as "sick" or to separate us from others thought to be "well". None of us has ever needed to be locked up, isolated, told we were incurable, or treated as outcasts' (Re-evaluation Counseling 1991: 9). Indeed, research confirms that social exclusion can *cause* 'mental illness' (i.e. distress) and certainly prevent recovery (Barham and Hayward 1995; Warner 1985).

In nineteenth-century Europe and North America, psychiatrists treated only the 'mad', people who would now be considered 'psychotic'. In the 1930s, people who were depressed or anxious began to be admitted as voluntary 'in' or 'out' patients. Since then, the definition of 'mental illness' has got wider and wider, so that all sorts of emotional troubles and feelings are medicalised. People who consult their doctors about emotional problems are likely to be prescribed antidepressants (it used to be tranquillisers).

The Re-evaluation Counselling Communities have taken a stand against the use of psychiatric drugs (as well as electroshock therapy and psychosurgery), all of which are damaging to the brain (Read 2001; Re-evaluation Counseling 2002: 53). Drugs inhibit discharge and re-evaluation, preventing recovery from the hurts that underlie people's difficulties. The distress is still there, and the person now has another hurtful experience to discharge – being damped down by drugs. In addition, these drugs often have dangerous side-effects.

Many forms of counselling reject the assumptions and practices of biopsychiatry. We, and they, do not accept the concept of 'mental illness' and do not see medical training as particularly relevant to assisting distressed people. Distress does have a biological dimension, as do all states of mind. Perhaps the balance of neurotransmitters is upset in people who are chronically depressed or anxious. However, we have found in RC that the *causes* of distress are almost always hurtful life experiences. In RC we rely on the client's natural healing process. We have found that sufficient discharge and re-evaluation reduce, and eventually eliminate, chronic anxiety and depression. We therefore assume that any needed changes in brain chemistry have taken place naturally.

Psychoanalysis

Freud, the father of psychoanalysis, discovered that through talking to an attentive listener, people could be freed from the effects of things that have gone wrong early in life. Many approaches, RC included, have recognised the good effects of such communication. Although Freud was himself a doctor and never gave up that status in relation to his 'patients', many psychoanalysts were not doctors, and in most countries psychoanalysis developed in opposition to the medical model.

In his early work (with Breuer) Freud used 'catharsis', which involved unravelling, under hypnosis, the early roots of a symptom (Breuer and Freud 1955). It bore some relationship to discharge, but the expression of emotion was understood as incidental, not central. Distress recordings can be brought to awareness under hypnosis (which itself installs a recording of submission to the hypnotist), but not dissolved. In RC we have found that simply knowing about a distress recording is not sufficient to make it go away. As far as we know, there is no acknowledgement in psychoanalysis of the crucial role of discharge (other than talking) in recovery from past hurts.

Human goodness

Both Freud in his time, and present-day psychoanalysis, do not hold with a central postulate of RC (and of some other approaches), that human beings are inherently good and that our antisocial and destructive tendencies are the result of hurtful experiences (Freud 1957). According to psychoanalytic theory, destructive urges are inherent to human beings. Painful inner conflict between society (and society's mental representatives, such as the superego), and these basic urges, is considered inevitable. In contrast, RC theory holds that inner conflict is not an inevitable part of being human, and that there is no inherent opposition between (a rational) society and human nature.

With some variation, the different schools of psychoanalysis tend to be pessimistic about what therapy can hope to achieve. By bringing much that is unconscious to awareness, inner conflict may be reduced but cannot be done away with. (Freud once said that psychoanalysis could hope to replace neurotic misery with 'ordinary unhappiness': Lieberman 1997.) Re-evaluation Counselling puts forth a very positive perspective: that with enough time and resource, the enjoyment of life, close and loving relationships with others, and 'genius-sized' capabilities can be *fully recovered*.

The unconscious

The unconscious mind is a crucial concept in psychoanalytic thinking. RC theory would say that at any given time, some of our thinking and feeling are at the level of awareness, some can be called to awareness, and some cannot be brought to awareness because of internal obstacles (and/or lack of external resource). There is no concept of a separate, dynamic unconscious. Memories and information become occluded and unavailable as a result of hurtful experiences, and exert an influence on a person unless he or she can recover from those experiences. Degrees of occlusion vary – in a session, memories and feelings may be noticed which are usually unavailable.

> Great portions of most clients' intelligences have been locked away, occluded, or 'buried' with the content of heavy distress recordings, and a kind of frozen

numbness entered into in these areas in order to allow the remaining intelligence to be free to handle the person's living situation as best it can.

(Jackins 1997: 56)

One way to access occluded distresses is by fantasising.

> In general it is not useful to suggest to the client that the fantasy must be similar to the suspected memory. Such stories can be about the client himself or herself, or about another imaginary person (or any other creature or entity).
>
> (Jackins 1997: 56)

Harvey remarks that when there is an early decision *not to know*, this decision has to be undone. The client can also decide to no longer be limited by the effects of this occluded distress, which makes it more available for discharge.

Sexuality

In the late 1890s, Freud recognised that the sexual abuse of children was both common and harmful (Freud 1962). However, within a few years he abandoned the view that people are hurt by what happens to them (in his terms, that abuse can cause neurosis). He then believed that people suffer from inner conflict between their own unconscious wishes (often sexual in nature) and internalised prohibitions. The theory of infantile sexuality is often hailed as the true beginning of psychoanalysis (Rycroft 1984) and is one of many places where psychoanalysis differs from RC (New 1996).

According to psychoanalytic theory, sexuality is the basic truth of relationships, so that friendship or affectionate relationships (for example, between parents and children) are 'aim-inhibited'. That is, their passion is supposed to come from their repressed sexual content. RC offers a different perspective. Babies' enthusiastic love and their desire for close and loving contact with their parents are natural human feelings which do not derive from sexuality. They become sexualised (leading to the idea of 'Oedipus') in societies or under conditions that permit passion and physical closeness only to sexual partners (or when there has been sexual abuse). As anthropologist Malinowski (1960) pointed out in correspondence with Freud, the Oedipal jealousy a little boy might feel toward his father in European society is probably related to that society's organisation of the nuclear family.

Freud tended to see the many varieties of sexual impulses as part of an individual's basic nature (the id). In 'A Rational Theory of Sexuality' Harvey Jackins (1981c) recognised that babies and young children naturally explore their bodies and enjoy their sensations, and that around puberty and adolescence there is an upsurge of sexual interest, curiosity and exploration. Sexual feelings are part of our human nature, but unless we are hurt, we are free to decide when it makes sense to act on them. Sexual compulsions (and inhibitions) are distress recordings laid in by hurtful experiences. Harvey described distress about sex as having been 'systematically imposed and enforced upon us in our cultures [so] that it covers everything . . . like a strip of sticky fly paper wound around our thinking, confusing and disturbing everything' (Jackins 1981c: 185).

One well-tested RC approach to discharging sexual distress is to review early memories connected in any way with sex. In general, we have found it useful to locate and discharge our *earliest* hurt on any chain of distresses (whether this be difficulties with relationships, food, taking tests, sex or whatever) and then focus on each memory in the chain of memories that follow, working extensively on the key ones. This approach can be especially useful in discharging distresses about sex because addressing these in terms of our present relationships and present-time feelings can be particularly confusing to client and counsellor.

It turns out that many of our triggers for sexual feelings are based in distress.

> If you review and discharge thoroughly . . . all your memories connected with sex in any way at all, you will see exactly where all your 'dear', 'familiar', 'rational' modes of sexuality arose. And they will all disappear, and . . . you may go through a period of wondering if you haven't 'ruined' this, until now, dependably push-buttoned area of your life.
>
> (Jackins 1981c: 98)

Recovery

Psychoanalytic therapy involves free association, in which the patient, who usually lies on a couch unable to see the analyst, says whatever comes into her or his mind. The analyst will occasionally interpret what has been said by showing its relationship to the transference, i.e. the relationship between analyst and patient in which the latter projects early feelings towards the parents onto the analyst. Interpretations are considered successful if they result in insight on the part of the patient. A psychoanalyst attempts to offer a blank screen to the patient, so that the patient is not steered away from work on early issues by the intrusion of anything related to the analyst's life. These precepts are all contested in psychoanalysis, and Freud's own practice was inconsistent, but such is the general consensus.

In RC, a client will often be talking in ways that could be called free association. There are times when an RC counsellor might *specifically* encourage a client (perhaps one who is heavily self-censoring) to say *whatever* is in her or his mind. However, it should also be noted that the RC client and counsellor are not in any way restricted to this format. Either and both take a variety of initiatives for the purpose of bringing about discharge of the distresses that are being addressed.

An RC counsellor does not interpret for the client. He or she is confident that, once freed by discharge to do so, the client's mind will spontaneously sort through the previously mis-stored information and make sense of it (re-evaluate). An RC counsellor will offer contradictions to the client's distress which are specifically designed to enable that particular client to see her or his distress as *distress* rather than present-day reality and as a result bring discharge.

In RC, too, some of the most effective work is done when a client uses his or her relationship with the counsellor to notice distresses and access discharge. It is clear that feelings from early times are frequently transferred on to others, including on to Co-Counsellors. In RC, we consider such transference to be a form of restimulation (being reminded of), which we can work on in our sessions (Somers 1972). This restimulation can be used to discharge tensions and hurts from earlier relationships. It often works well to contradict distress recordings by reaching for the necessarily different and unhurtful reality of the present-time relationship. When a Co-Counselling client speaks of or shows strong feelings about his or her counsellor, the counsellor might ask, 'Who is it that I remind you of? What's the similarity? How am I different from that person (for example, your mother)?' Then the client talks and perhaps cries or laughs (and so on) about the similarities and differences, draining tension from old hurts and at the same time becoming clearer that the counsellor is separate from these restimulations.

The security of present-time relationships can be used to mourn what was missing in earlier times and to eventually remember with love and gratitude good memories and good intentions of people from long ago. To do this effectively, the client needs encouragement to let old feelings come up and discharge, and the contradiction of the counsellor's real, present-time love. The no-socialising and confidentiality guidelines help create the safety for this to happen (see Chapter 5).

We have found that the existence of the Re-evaluation Counselling Communities makes a difference to what can be accomplished in individual Co-Counselling sessions, by providing additional resources of attention and skill from a wide variety of people, as well as encouragement, new theory, continuity, connection and safety.

Behavioural approaches

Behavioural approaches developed in the 1940s as applications of classical learning theory and laboratory work on conditioning. In their early forms they were reductionist and mechanical. We would say in RC that these methods were based in the aspects of our nature that we share with other living creatures, not in what is specifically human. Behavioural therapists used rewards and punishments to try to change their clients' unwanted behaviour. 'Token economies' were used (and to some extent still are) in mental hospitals to bring about desired behaviour by patients. 'Grounds privileges' or the right to go to the hospital café are still used to reward behaviour that is deemed appropriate. Unlike RC, a close caring relationship between the counsellor and the client was not seen as crucial.

According to behaviour modification theory, anxiety, phobias and other painful feelings are conditioned responses to certain stimuli (not the result of stored hurtful experiences, as understood in RC). Therapy is aimed at breaking the link to the stimuli by means of 'desensitising' techniques (Gregory 1987; Wachtel 1977).

Behavioural approaches focus on the goal of changing discrete behaviours. Clients who could not fly in aeroplanes are enabled to fly. People who could not leave the house are enabled to do so. People who could not stop washing their hands manage to stop.

In the 1960s and 1970s, rational emotive behaviour therapy and later cognitive behaviour therapy (CBT) broke from the mechanistic model of conditioning and acknowledged the effect of people's beliefs and feelings. Roughly speaking, they aim to assist clients to identify irrational beliefs, to see them as irrational and to become free of them. The 'schemata' identified in CBT sound like what we call distress recordings: 'I must always perform well', 'The world is a dangerous and overwhelming place' (Dobson 2000).

Similar to CBT, as RC clients we do our best to align our behaviour with our best thinking (often in opposition to feelings that push us to behave irrationally). This will generally bring up feelings that are then discharged.

Behavioural therapists argue firmly with the pattern and encourage their clients to do so. RC clients and counsellors *contradict* patterns in any way they can think of in order to bring about the discharge of the pattern. Once in a while contradicting a pattern may look like arguing with it.

Behavioural methods have also had success in identifying – as we would put it – how people collude with each other's distresses, and in devising strategies for interrupting this 'hooking'. From an RC point of view, these gains are made by harnessing the client's power to think and decide. RC counsellors do something similar when they support the client in acting outside the pattern, which leads to better functioning and constitutes an effective contradiction to the distress. However, in RC we also aim for sustained discharge of the hurts that underlie the fears and compulsions. CBT does not emphasise or encourage discharge as far as we know. We might speculate that when permanent gains are made using CBT, the client has been able to discharge in some way.

Co-Counsellors have had considerable success using the power of decision to make changes in their behaviour and lives, but in our experience, to actually eliminate a hurt and its effects, discharge is required. The relationship between decision and discharge is still being explored. Harvey Jackins asked:

> How much is it possible to act on decision alone, regardless of the remaining distress? How exhaustive and complete is it necessary for discharge to be before the new course of action can be effective and permanent? What seems certain is that the interaction between choosing and deciding against the pattern, and the permanent removal of the pattern through exhaustive discharge, are both re-emergent processes, that they support each other, and that neither process must be postponed for or 'wait for' the other.
>
> (Jackins 1997: 27)

Humanistic approaches

At a meeting with counsellors and therapists in Seattle in October 1972, Harvey Jackins remarked:

> [I]n a ... general sense there's no doubt that we [i.e. RC] are part of a movement toward a more humanistic approach to people, the humanist psychology movement. We're very happy to pay tribute to the giants of humanistic psychology who have broken trail and broken company with the inhuman attitudes of the past, such people as Maslow and Perls and Rogers ... We don't feel we have learned from them or borrowed from them; we've tried to remain completely independent.
>
> (Jackins 1972)

Humanistic psychology developed in the 1940s and 1950s as a 'third force' distinct from psychoanalysis and behaviourism (Rowan 1976). Its basic assumption is that human beings are, by their species nature, inherently good, and have an inherent capacity for self-healing. Abraham Maslow writes: 'Destructiveness, sadism, cruelty, malice, and so on, seem so far to be not intrinsic but rather ... violent reactions against frustration of our inner needs, emotions, and capacities' (Maslow 1968: 3).

Re-evaluation Counselling shares the assumption of basic human goodness. Somers writes that the counsellor's use of this concept is made more powerful by his or her 'own experience in contacting his or her core self through the continuing process' (Somers 1972: 3).

Re-evaluation Counselling and humanistic psychology face similar criticisms from those who ask on what grounds we describe prosocial cooperative impulses as 'natural' and 'real'. Critics argue that since human beings must be capable of whatever they do, violence and antisocial activity must themselves be part of human nature (New 1996). We would answer that such behaviour is not characteristic of humans until we have been at the receiving end of hurtful experiences; therefore, it is not part of our *inherent* underlying nature. Humans feel badly (grief, fear, rage and so on) when we are mistreated, and these feelings discharge spontaneously if allowed to. When discharge is not permitted, the human tendency to reproduce elements of a hurtful experience in our behaviour makes it easy to confuse the rigid recordings 'attached' to a person with that person's inherent self.

Re-evaluation Counselling shares with humanistic approaches a refusal to focus on pathology, on what is 'wrong' with a person, or to use the language of abnormal psychology. It is truthful and more useful to regard every client as already functioning well in some respects and struggling in others. To make what is 'wrong' the starting point, instead of starting with and noticing the intact inherent *person*, can lead to disrespectful and counterproductive treatment (similar to when hospital staff refer to 'the lungs in bed six' and 'the appendectomy in bed nine').

Distress is not illness or disease, and categorising people in terms of their distresses is not helpful to them. We may note some similarities in the ways human beings respond to similar sorts of hurt, but as counsellors we recognise that in spite of these appearances, each client has suffered unique hurts under specific circumstances and needs to be counselled accordingly. Labels such as 'borderline personality disorder' or 'schizophrenic' get in the way of the counsellor seeing the client as an intact human being who is operating under the influence of particular hurts and life circumstances. Labels mislead and make it harder to think well and precisely about the individual.

Humanistic approaches (mostly) hold that it is possible to build societies that fit with human nature. Maslow uses the term 'synergy' to describe institutional arrangements in which 'the individual by the same act and at the same time serves his own advantage and that of the group' (Maslow 1973: 210). Harvey Jackins goes further: 'No individual human being has an actual rational conflict of interest with another human. Given rationality, the actual desires of each can best be served by mutual co-operation' (Jackins 1983b: 329). (Jackins is talking about people as distinct from their patterns.) Fritz Perls, the founder of Gestalt, wrote that the current organisation of society 'has undergone a process that has moved it so far from healthy functioning that our needs and the needs of society and the needs of nature do not fit together any more' (Perls 1972: 18). As noted earlier, RC recognises the effects of social structure in the production and maintenance of distress patterns, and also that oppressive societies depend for their continuation on chronic patterns.

The counsellor's attitude

Carl Rogers, founder of person centred counselling, held that 'unconditional positive regard' is the right and effective attitude for the counsellor to have toward the client. This means that counsellors need to be 'freely and deeply' themselves. '[I]t is the opposite of presenting a façade, either knowingly or unknowingly' (Rogers 1990: 224). He emphasises that 'unconditional positive regard' must really *be* unconditional – the counsellor must accept negative feelings and inconsistency in the client. Rogers talks about the counsellor genuinely accepting the client as she or he now is, and without (for instance) feelings of revulsion toward some of what the client says.

Harvey Jackins describes seven attitudes of an effective counsellor. These are approval, delight and respect; confidence in, and for, the client; relaxed (not anxious or pressured) high expectations of the client; and love for the client (Jackins 1997: 44). RC's clear distinction between the person and the pattern is relevant here. We always try to maintain a positive attitude toward the inherent human being. We can hold on to the theoretical knowledge (sometimes under intense provocation, depending on what is restimulative to us as counsellors) that the intact human really exists and is completely separate from how, for example, he or she might be acting. Then, always warmly supporting the *person*, we are free to take any attitude toward the pattern that will assist in its demise. We can even take a murderous attitude toward it; after all, it has made our client's life difficult. We have to be able to make the separation clearly enough that the client is not attacked or invalidated when we 'attack' the pattern. We *simultaneously* remember who the person really is and put everything at our disposal into demolishing the recording.

The clearer the counsellor is about the distinction between the person and the pattern, and the more he or she has discharged (so as not to be upset by the client's patterns and thus be made reactive and inflexible), the more effective he or she will be.

What counsellors do

Rogers speaks of being on the side of the client and trusts that the client's inner wisdom will move him or her to where he or she needs to go. Co-Counsellors keep in mind that to be on the side of the client is to *not be on the side of the client's patterns*. As clients we tend to confuse ourselves with our patterns, and we sometimes try to get our counsellors to agree that our patterned attitudes and behaviour make sense. As counsellors, we can't go along with this and be useful to our clients. Distress recordings were installed on us under great duress, were the only 'solution' we could come up with at the time, and seemed to make survival possible. Therefore, even now in a very different present, as clients we can feel that it's dangerous to challenge them. Counsellors must figure out how to make it so clear to the client that they are completely *for* him or her, that when they take initiatives to oppose (contradict) the pattern, the client will have the safety to allow feelings to come up and to let them discharge.

As in most humanistic approaches, the Co-Counselling client is the only authority about himself or herself. It is the client who discharges and comes to understand the origins of his or her distressed feelings and ways of acting. In general, the counsellor does not express opinions about what the client should think or do in his or her life. A counsellor offers his or her thinking if it seems that a voice from outside will act as a contradiction and elicit discharge, thus enabling the client to find his or her own thinking. When the counsellor shows all the important attitudes, the client's own mind will generally present what needs to be worked on and will tend to furnish its own contradictions. Then discharge and re-evaluation happen spontaneously.

Often a counsellor just needs to be fully present, which in itself is a contradiction to many distresses. When the client's chronic distress recording obscures some aspect of reality and the counsellor's presence does not sufficiently contradict it, then the counsellor needs to be more active. What the counsellor says or does is usually built on what the client has already said. For example, when I (Caroline) was trying to facilitate discharge for an English person who was describing her chronic paralysing guilt in relation to Irish people, I asked in an intentionally naive tone at what point she reckoned she had begun oppressing the

Irish? Was there any chance that at least the sperm and egg that came together to make her had been innocent? She laughed a lot. I asked her if she had been part of Cromwell's invasion, and she laughed more. This was just one of many possible things that could have been said to elicit discharge, in the context of a warm human relationship.

In many counselling approaches the counsellor will reflect back to the client what she or he has been saying. An RC counsellor might at times reflect back to a client, but the RC counsellor would do so only if it would lead the client to discharge (not because the counsellor thought that the client needed to hear this for any other reason).

Self-disclosure

Humanistic approaches permit, in some circumstances, the counsellor's 'self-disclosure'. Because client and counsellor roles are exchanged in RC, the client does not need the counsellor's self-disclosure in order to be aware of the coun-sellor's real, separate existence. As counsellors, we need not conceal the details of our lives from clients (as in psychoanalysis). In the counsellor role, we would say something about ourselves only if it promised to help the client discharge. For example, 'You are important to me'. Such a statement would draw the client's attention to the reality of the relationship.

In RC we have moved from seeing restimulation as something that *happens to us*, as external and hard to control as the weather, to seeing it as involving a degree of choice. When we are counsellors, we may have to make and remake the decision not to be restimulated – which means deciding and redeciding not to confuse the client and the current situation and relationship with something in our own past. Inevitably counsellors will sometimes be restimulated and sometimes be unaware that they are acting on restimulation. For example, someone told me (Caroline) that when he was counselling an older woman, he didn't challenge her limited perspective because he felt that at her age she had 'earned a rest'. (He later realised he had unawarely assumed a distressed perspective based on stereotyped attitudes toward older people.)

When, as counsellors, we notice that we cannot listen in a relaxed way to what our client is saying, or are urgently pulled to offer directions, opinions or advice, we might tell our client that we are restimulated (it is better to admit it than to pretend) and ask him or her to be counsellor for a few minutes. Incidentally, the counsellor's openness about restimulation, and his or her determination to overcome it so as to be truly present, sometimes move the client to discharge.

Tangentially related to self-disclosure, Co-Counsellors often meet on the basis of a commonality, such as age, gender, background or heritage. As people in the group openly reveal (i.e. 'disclose') how the commonly held 'identity' has affected them, it creates safety and leads to each person's deeper understanding of his or her own experience, and to discharge.

Another model of peer counselling

The term 'Co-Counselling' was appropriated (much against Harvey Jackins' wishes) and continues to be used by an organisation which separated from RC in the 1960s, Co-Counseling International (CCI).

Since CCI originated in RC, there are overlaps between its core model and RC theory. Among the differences with RC, CCI networks do not operate like the RC Communities – for example, disagreement with RC's notion of leadership (see Chapter 9) was a factor in CCI's decision to split off. The no-socialising guideline is less firm in CCI. Also, CCI separated from RC before the theory of oppression and liberation was well developed, which may explain why CCI does not consider societal oppression to be a major source of distress recordings, or personal re-emergence to be bound up with social liberation.

Summary

Since therapists and counsellors have been grappling with the same human realities as we have in Re-evaluation Counselling, they have necessarily noticed some of the same phenomena, resulting in some parallel concepts. However, Re-evaluation Counselling is a distinct approach to human recovery from distress, with its own assumptions, and its own internally consistent, well-tested theory and practice.

Although limited by experience, time and space, we hope we have given an adequate summary of some key features of a few other approaches, to enable readers to better understand Re-evaluation Counselling. We want to take this opportunity to appreciate therapists and counsellors, their caring, and their hard work on behalf of their fellow human beings.

Chapter 9

Advancing theory in Re-evaluation Counselling

I had no notion of where this was going . . . so a good deal of the early progress was what the mathematicians call a drunkard's walk. It was good because we did move . . . Once in a while we saw a gleam of light [and] as we got enough gleams of light, the theory began to be put together . . . This is the way it evolved, and this is the way any important theory evolves.

(H. Jackins 2003: 5, from a 1971 talk)

I (Katie) found my way to Re-evaluation Counselling in 1968, just as the theory and practice were spreading beyond Seattle. By the time I began participating, the basic theory had already been extrapolated from consistent results with many people, and had been guiding a practice for over fifteen years. A hundred or more people in Seattle, USA, were Co-Counselling, as well as participating in fundamentals and intermediate classes. A professional staff at Personal Counselors, Inc. (the founding and research centre for the development of Re-evaluation Counselling) had, for some time, been offering one-way Re-evaluation Counselling for a fee in order to continue the systematic research and to provide funds for the project. There was already a collection of literature about the process and practice – the basic theory as described in *The Human Side of Human Beings* (Jackins 1965) and the *Fundamentals of Co-Counseling Manual* (Personal Counselors 1962), and a few pamphlets.

Over the next several decades, Harvey Jackins and his associates proceeded to apply the fundamental theory to a wide variety of situations and problems. A few attempts were quickly discarded as unworkable (Harvey comments on these in *The List*), but most innovations served to advance the theory and practice.

The Re-evaluation Counselling Communities

The Re-evaluation Counselling Communities began to take shape in the early 1970s. Since then, theoretical developments have taken place within the context of this loosely organised group of people. We will briefly describe the structure and functioning of the RC Communities.

As early as the late 1960s, Co-Counsellors – whose numbers by that time were increasing – began spontaneously to meet together for purposes that did not fit neatly into Co-Counselling session or class formats. Structures were needed to make additional group relationships work well, structures that would support individual re-emergence from distress. In proposing these forms, Harvey Jackins tried to avoid bureaucratic or otherwise cumbersome aspects of other organisations. What evolved was a network of Co-Counsellors organised with minimal structure.

I (Katie) remember when, in about 1970, Harvey was communicating with Co-Counsellors, originally from Seattle, who had moved to other parts of the country. They wanted to continue Co-Counselling and needed Co-Counsellors for themselves. They wanted to be able to teach classes. To ensure that RC would be taught accurately, procedures were developed for approving and certifying new RC teachers.

Growth continued and along with it the need for additional formats and organisational forms. Within a ten-year period, workshops, support groups, leaders' groups and conferences were added to the already existing fundamentals and intermediate classes. As Co-Counsellors became teachers of Co-Counselling, clear guidelines for leadership were needed, and a theory of leadership evolved. Publications proliferated, especially for particular constituencies.

There is a single requirement for participation in the Re-evaluation Counselling Communities – called the 'one-point programme' – and this is to seek recovery of one's own occluded intelligence and assist others to do the same. Co-Counsellors who consider themselves RC Community members also participate in Co-Counselling classes and workshops and agree to follow the *Guidelines of the Re-evaluation Counseling Communities* (Re-evaluation Counseling 2002). All Co-Counsellors are encouraged to join with other Co-Counsellors in seeking intelligent positions on all issues facing humanity, including the most controversial ones. It is not necessary to *agree with* any of these positions in order to be a member in good standing in the RC Community.

> All our policies are draft policies. They are not presented as dogma but as our best thinking to date. They may be right and they may be wrong. When they are most controversial, people will have to keep discharging on them to reveal their irrationality or clarity. If, over time, the policies help people discharge and seem to reflect reality, we keep them. If not, we re-evaluate and discard them. However, even if we keep them, no one should be pressured by the group or by any leader to agree with what they say.
>
> (Brown 1999: 20)

Areas, which are geographically based, were the earliest organisational structure to evolve. An Area is led by an Area Reference Person, chosen by local Co-Counsellors through a process of thinking and discharging to reach consensus. The Area Reference Person's overall function is to exercise judgement about

Co-Counselling activities in the area. Later, Areas were organised into Regions, and Regional Reference Persons were appointed by the International Reference Person. About the same time, Liberation Reference Persons (based on function rather than geography, for constituencies such as women, men, Native people, elders, trade unionists) were appointed. The Liberation Reference Person's job is to think about the members of his or her constituency and to encourage leadership, policies, writing, workshops and conferences which address this group's liberation.

The above are unpaid positions, although leaders are paid for teaching classes and leading workshops.

Policies are updated every four years at a world conference, and the International Reference Person and Alternate International Reference Person are confirmed (or not) in their posts until the next world conference. The goals for the next four years are discussed in the light of suggestions and amendments received from the RC Communities during the preparatory period.

Leadership

When possible, decisions are made by consensus, arrived at by taking turns thinking and listening. Routine day-to-day decisions or those needing speedy resolution can be made by the leader. A model of *individual leadership* has worked well. At least one person needs to think about the group as a whole (not only about his or her individual role in it), about its origins and direction, and about its individual members. He or she does not do the thinking *for* the group, but instead listens well to participants and brings their own ideas back to them in the form of proposals for new initiatives. One person (not two people or a committee of people) is clearly responsible for a given sphere of activity, and is backed and assisted by others. 'At least one person in a group must think of the group as a whole if that group is to function well. It is excellent and very workable if more than one does' (Jackins 1987: 5).

Clear leadership responsibility facilitates decision-making and reduces the likelihood of vacillation and non-productive debate. Decisions can be quickly made and put into effect. If a decision turns out to be mistaken, feedback from putting it into effect will reveal this. Because the discharge and re-evaluation process is built into RC deliberations, it is often possible to peel off people's fears, feelings of urgency, antagonisms, eagerness for attention or prominence and so on, so that these do not dominate policy discussions and meetings.

The RC Communities have focused considerable attention on leadership, not only because leaders are needed to carry on the work, but also because leadership is a human capacity and because individuals (and worthy projects) benefit greatly when this capacity is fully recovered. Harvey Jackins (1987: 4) emphasised that 'every person is a potential leader' and that 'to achieve this potential is part of the complete development of the intelligence of every human'. Co-Counsellors are encouraged to lead when they are ready, and are supported while they learn.

Harvey Jackins was the International Reference Person for the Re-evaluation Counselling Communities from their beginnings until his death in 1999. His Co-Counselling relationships with (a very large number of) people were a strong support to their being able to take on the challenges of teaching and leading. Harvey could be easily reached by phone and email, and, when Co-Counsellors made new discoveries in the theory and practice, they would communicate these directly to him. He would then put the best discoveries forward as proposals for new theory and practice, and consult widely and thoroughly for feedback. For example, before writing *The List* (1997), Harvey consulted hundreds of RC leaders in many countries, whose thinking contributed to the final book.

Proposals for new theory, practice and policy are widely discussed in the Re-evaluation Counselling Communities. The promising ideas are put into practice so that results can be evaluated. If these ideas meet the test of consistency with the basic theory, and the results are uniformly productive and interesting, their usefulness will be made known in classes, workshops and publications (and, in the past, in phone sessions with Harvey in which he often tried out new ideas). Successful ideas become part of the body of collected experience and are incorporated into standard practice. It's important to note that this ferment of ideas occurs among people who are both close and connected through their Co-Counselling relationships, and who have also learned how to listen well to each other's thinking; these factors have undoubtedly played a part in the large output and quality of new ideas.

The role played by the leader, as described above, is one example of well-functioning leadership. Leadership theory and practices consistent with RC assumptions have been collected, articulated and passed on by modelling and the written word.

An RC leader writes about her early experience of leading in RC:

> Although I could get by when speaking to almost any group outside of Co-Counselling, I froze when I tried to give RC theory to my new group of eight very sweet, good people. Why was that? It was because I knew that to reach people in an RC class, I had to be present emotionally . . . I don't remember feeling terror like that except when I was three. I was learning my first lesson about RC leadership: Stretching hard allows heavy undischarged feelings to come up.
>
> (Brown 1999: 5)

She goes on to describe how as a result of challenging her chronic distresses through leading inside RC, her life and leadership outside RC have flourished.

Handling disagreements

Like most, if not all, large organisations that exist for decades, the RC Community has had many people be critical of its ideas and functioning. Some of this criticism has come from people who knew very little about Re-evaluation Counselling and some from people who were involved with it. Some participants in the RC Community have left because of disagreements, while others have been able to resolve matters and remain, and even play leading roles.

Most people carry distresses about organisations and leaders, and often criticisms contain restimulations of earlier distress experiences. The opportunity to counsel on the earlier incidents often makes it possible for people to improve their communication, and to resolve any actual disagreements. When disagreements have involved people outside the RC Community, these people have not had the same opportunity to work on the related distresses, and so resolution has been more difficult and sometimes not possible. In RC, we have been able to develop policies to guide Co-Counsellors through confusing restimulations to the resolution of the real issues.

RC policies for handling disagreements include:

- talking about the issues, not the people involved
- working in sessions on the emotional upsets so that they do not cloud discussion of the issues
- speaking directly to the person with whom one has a disagreement (rather than gossiping or complaining to others), and if the disagreement is not resolved, consulting an RC Reference Person
- supporting people to propose better policies rather than to criticise an individual.

Real difficulties do arise, of course, and mistakes are made in RC. In general, we assume that mistakes are not made intentionally or maliciously, but are due to having different information and perspectives and, very often, from having distresses interfere with one's thinking.

There have been attempts to limit the availability of Re-evaluation Counselling (and other forms of non-professional counselling) to the general population (House and Totton 1997). These efforts to regulate counselling have been made mainly by people who earn their livings as therapists and appear to have an economic root. For example, in the mid-1980s, degreed counsellors, psychologists and social workers in Washington State (USA) lobbied for a bill in the Washington State Legislature to restrict the right to counsel to people with master's degrees. As part of this campaign, attempts were made to denigrate all non-professionalised counselling. (The legislation failed.)

Developing theory

We have mentioned the decision to develop RC independently of other approaches to human recovery. Harvey Jackins had a background in science, valued scientific methods, and was a philosophical realist (Jackins 1973a: 62). The early decision to base and build the theory only on what he and his colleagues learned from direct experience meant not being influenced by other theories and not automatically accepting the 'common sense' of the time. All points of theory were questioned and tested extensively before being accepted. The aim was to build an internally consistent, externally valid theory and a reliable and effective practice.

If phenomena were observed many times, they were assumed to be general tendencies and were made part of the theory – Harvey called this the 'inductive structure'. In the early 1960s he and his colleagues also summed up what was known in the form of twenty-four Postulates or assumptions, which were consistent with each other and with what had been observed, and had implications for what could be expected to be observed in the future. New developments in the theory were scrutinised for consistency with this deductive structure, and its assumptions continued to be 'checked against reality'.

Harvey Jackins insisted that theories consist of conjectures from generalisations from observations – not of 'laws'. He recognised the provisional nature of theory.

> The theory that we call Re-evaluation Counseling is not necessarily the only explanation that could be made about successful counseling practice. It is simply the best guesses that we have been able to make as to why these successes happen . . . any part of RC theory is subject to revision at any time that real, verified evidence contradicts it.
>
> (Jackins 1978b: 80)

Modifications of basic theory

Restimulation

Since its early formulation, there have few additions to or updates in the most basic theory (which we have described in Chapters 1 to 6 of this book). One change was a refinement in the understanding of restimulation (the triggering-of-earlier-hurts 'mechanism'). With a closer look, it was determined that restimulation is not something completely beyond our control (as Co-Counsellors were sometimes assuming to their detriment). Being upset by events in the present because of their similarity to past hurts and, especially, acting on these upset feelings, leads to not handling the present well. However, the triggering mechanism can be largely brought under our control. Understanding the phenomenon, and with a place to take our feelings (for Co-Counsellors, to Co-Counselling sessions), we can more often resist using restimulation as a way to access feelings. Instead, we can systematically dismantle our distresses in a cleaner and more efficient way – without adding problems to our lives by upsetting others, and with a counsellor there to assist us.

We can decide ahead of time not to be upset in circumstances that in the past brought on overwhelming feelings and unintelligent actions. For example, once we realise that being criticised is a trigger for early distresses, before going into situations where we can expect to be criticised, we can have a session or two in which we practise (and discharge about) *deciding not to be restimulated* by criticism. Then we can go to that situation and handle it instead of being overcome with upset feelings. We will also need sessions in which we discharge hurts from past criticism so that they no longer exert a pull on us to be restimulated.

The above clarification helped people to be less helpless in the face of restimulation.

Contradiction

'Contradiction' was an important early concept that was later understood and articulated more clearly. Harvey Jackins wrote in 1993:

> In the last two years, after realizing the central importance of the concept of 'contradiction,' we have been able to relate all of the successful past approaches ('techniques') of counseling to a general framework. All . . . can be seen as some form or other of applying the 'contradiction principle' in a session. By contradiction we mean anything that allows the victim or bearer of the pattern to realize that the pattern is NOT present time reality. When a distress pattern is thus 'contradicted,' and the contradiction is persisted in, the pattern becomes converted to discharge.
>
> (Jackins 1993b: 15)

Reality and pseudo-reality

Cumulative RC experience has resulted in a clearer understanding of the distinction between reality and distress. Misrepresentations of reality (for example, the idea that humans are inherently and inevitably destructive and competitive) not only arise from distress but also produce additional distress. Harvey Jackins suggested the term 'pseudo-reality' for such misrepresentations. 'Present human traditions, relationships, institutions, politics, and educational and health care systems are all heavily contaminated by distress patterns' (Jackins 1997: 8). The concept of a distinction between reality and pseudo-reality is useful in our daily lives. With this concept we are better able to see discouraging misrepresentations for what they are.

Chronic distresses

An early advance in the theory was the recognition that intermittent and chronic distresses differ in the amount of hurt they contain and that they require different counselling strategies. (We discussed this in detail in Chapter 3.)

Eliminating chronic distress recordings continues to be one of the most challenging tasks we humans confront. In recent years the RC Community has arrived at a clearer understanding of the pervasiveness and depth of human hurt.

We now know it usually takes considerable resource – of attention, skill, and time – to completely discharge chronic patterns. In the early 1970s, when our collective experience was still limited, I (Katie) remember that freedom from chronic distresses was sometimes spoken of as 'just around the corner.'

Tim Jackins writes:

> Human beings have never had a chance to be completely themselves, ever. No humans ever survived to the point where they could maintain themselves with being human still fully within their grasp. We get to try to do this. It's the hope we had as children for what life and relationships could be.
>
> (T. Jackins 2003: 25)

Advancing RC theory includes a number of new strategies for discharging chronic distress. For example, in the 1990s Harvey Jackins experimented with taking attention *completely off distress* as one of many ways to access discharge. The client and counsellor agree to deal only with the rational and benign aspects of the world, persons or situations. No matter what confusing problem or painful emotion preoccupied the client, he or she would not spend any time talking about it, nor looking back to early experiences related to the difficulties. Instead, clients would think and talk about people they love or who love them, about their own goodness, about the beauty of the world, and so on.

> I think that this gives us access to the tremendous ability of the client's mind to discharge, re-evaluate, and think when it is not hobbled by rehearsing the distresses which have claimed part of its attention in most past sessions.
>
> (Jackins 1993b: 21)

Co-Counsellors throughout the communities experimented with this way of working, and reported on their findings in *Present Time*.

In Re-evaluation Counselling we have had considerable success in discharging chronic patterns. As the pattern becomes less chronic, it no longer feels like a natural part of ourselves. It may still be restimulated, but will no longer 'play' all the time. We can see Co-Counsellors' facial expressions become more open and relaxed, as their chronic patterns loosen their hold.

Isolation

Harvey Jackins pointed out that our human nature includes the expectation that we will enjoy closeness with other intelligences as part of our normal living. However, this expectation is generally denied, beginning with the circumstances attending birth and later by many other factors.

> There has been heavy conditioning (and training) of almost all of us to be isolated from other people, to not trust other people, to assume that we must

be essentially lonely . . . I am conjecturing that every one of us probably has a deep, deep need to not spend any more of our life isolated and separate.

(Jackins 1993c: 86)

Harvey found that most clients discharge at the idea of being completely close to their counsellors.

Isolation is hurtful in and of itself, but it also impedes our recovery from other distresses. We are better able to face the intensely uncomfortable feelings that accompany the contradiction and discharge of chronic patterns when we are close and connected to another person.

By the late 1990s, RC had advanced its understanding of the widespread nature of isolation and of the hurts and patterns caused by it. We have put increasing emphasis on contradicting and discharging these patterns.

Patterns of isolation can be particularly strong in some cultures, religious traditions and social classes, for example, in some forms of Protestantism, and in the middle and owning classes. Ruth's (1998) work in RC has uncovered links between chronic feelings of isolation and being valued conditionally for one's work or good behaviour rather than for oneself, as often occurs in the afore-mentioned groups.

Tim Jackins writes: 'Rigid oppressive societies stay in place by keeping people from being close to each other. We couldn't tolerate what society does to other people if we were close to them' (T. Jackins 2002: 3).

We have discovered that we can accelerate our discharge of distress by ending our isolation from people of different class backgrounds, ages, ethnicities and so on. Among other things, a close relationship with someone from another group pushes us to get a clearer picture of reality. It also makes us aware of the limiting distresses of our own group and thereby makes these distresses more available for discharge.

Recovery from distress is also enhanced when we address it as more than just a personal endeavour. Among its many contributions to recovery, the RC Community counters and contradicts isolation. We have found that re-emergence from individual distress is accelerated by making it a collective project.

Recent work on 'inclusion' reflects, in part, our growing understanding of the depth of isolation that is built into our societies. Certain people have been ignored and excluded – for example, homeless people, disabled people and people in prisons. Inclusion workshops bring together people who have been generally accepted in mainstream society and those who have been separated and excluded from it (Mason 2002). Being separated from any group of people deprives the rest of us of the special strengths and insights into reality which that group has been able to retain.

Advances in work on oppression

Over a quarter of a century has passed since the theory of oppression and liberation was first formulated in RC.[1] We have gained an increasingly broad perspective in this area. We better understand the context in which we are working to recover from past distress.

This understanding of context has had a great influence on individual Co-Counselling sessions. For example, I (Katie) cannot ignore the fact that one of my Co-Counsellors was raised poor and that no matter what else she is working on, she is encased in a sense of failure and unworthiness due to having been treated disrespectfully as a poor person. Nor can I ignore that my Jewish Co-Counsellor feels the horror of the Holocaust hanging over him even though he had no direct experience of it.

A great deal of auxiliary theory developed around work on oppression. Throughout the 1970s, in Co-Counselling sessions, caucuses, workshops and support groups, information was gathered about successful work in this area. This theory and practice grew by leaps and bounds. A number of formats were designed to help people speak and discharge about the injustices they had been subject to, and to have these injustices understood and acknowledged by other Co-Counsellors.[2]

I (Caroline) remember when, in the early 1980s, we recognised that many groups are actually oppressed whom we had previously defined more narrowly as 'hurt'. In my first fundamentals class, men were described as *hurt*, while women were *oppressed*. As mentioned in Chapter 6, in the late 1980s we came to realise that men are also *systematically mistreated*. In the case of men there is no specific group of agents-of-oppression; the mechanisms of their oppression are built into social structures. With this advance came the understanding that other groups (such as parents, middle-class and even owning-class people) are also oppressed – again, not by a particular group acting as agent-of-oppression, but by the workings of society.

In recent years, our understanding of internalised oppression as it operates in particular groups has become deeper and more detailed. We can offer increasingly precise support to members of oppressed groups as they attempt to recognise and discharge their internalised oppression. In one initiative, Co-Counsellors were invited to determine and describe the essence of a particular internalised oppression by writing a short 'commitment' against it – in effect, a succinct draft policy statement countering it. For example, since women's internalised oppression usually involves submission to limitations, a commitment for women encourages them to decide and discharge in the direction of never again settling for anything less than 'absolutely' everything. A proposed commitment for young people highlights and contradicts the internalisation of the disrespect aimed at this group: 'I will never again treat any young person, including myself, with anything less than complete respect' (Jackins 1997: 9). Commitments were proposed for many constituencies and, in conjunction with a growing number of new insights and approaches, have facilitated decision, action and discharge.

We have come to understand that everybody has been oppressed, and everybody has played oppressor roles.

> Almost without exception, every person who has lived in our present oppressive societies has distress needing to be discharged from experiences of having been oppressed, *and also from experiences of having been in the oppressor role.*
>
> (Jackins 1997: 158 author's italic)

We have continued to develop ways of freeing ourselves from the distresses of both roles. One basic way to begin work on the oppressor role is to ask a client to remember and discharge about his or her first contact with someone belonging to the corresponding oppressed group (Jackins 1997: 159). It is particularly important that recordings of 'feeling bad about oneself' be rejected and contradicted as we work to free ourselves from the hurts of the oppressor role.

We have refined 'allies work', in which people who are not members of a particular oppressed group become good counsellors for those who are. In 1993, Harvey proposed that all of us think about and plan to be allies for others and to

> expand the numbers of people doing this until, at some time in the future, there will be no human being of any age or any other characteristic that does not have humans of different characteristics close at hand, ready to take initiative towards supporting her or him in her or his survival and goals.
>
> (Jackins 1993d: 186)

Deciding to oppose the oppression of another group, to counsel its members well, and to make close relationships among them, usually brings up feelings for the allies to discharge. These may be fears of being targeted themselves, or feelings that their own goodness depends on being approved of by the other group. Allies to particular groups find that their connection with these groups enriches their lives. They benefit from contact with whichever aspects of humanness the other group have been able to keep, despite their oppression.

Self-appreciation, hope and discharging racism

An early advance was clarifying the appropriateness and role of unlimited self-appreciation. Harvey and his associates noticed that self-appreciation often led to discharge, and they wondered how far humans could logically go in appreciating themselves. They concluded that we can appreciate ourselves (our inherent human selves, not our distress-based failures and foibles) *without any reservation whatsoever* because we always remain intact under our distresses and at any time in the past did the best we could, when all the circumstances are taken into account (Jackins 1973c).

Recently, complete self-appreciation has been systematically applied to the work of discharging patterns of white racism. We have found that counselling on these hurts becomes bogged down when white people focus on feelings of self-blame and guilt. What does work is to recognise one's inherent goodness and innocence and to discharge the oppressor role from that perspective. Tim Jackins encourages white people to be pleased with themselves *as part of the work*. 'If you aren't pleased with yourself, you're accepting part of what the oppressive society has done to you. You're accepting that pattern as you. This is incorrect' (T. Jackins 2000: 27). It has become clearer that feeling bad about ourselves actually serves the oppressive society by keeping us separate and powerless.

About the mistakes we've made, Tim says, 'I'm sorry you were part of the contagion that passes hurts along.' However,

> We have to fight to end racism, not because we are bad [we are not] but because ending it is essential for everyone, including ourselves . . . Facing racism is not going to easily feel good, but we get to be proud of doing it.
>
> (T. Jackins 2000a: 28)

We have found that it is realistic to be hopeful in connection with ending racism. For example, we have deliberately called our project 'United to *End* Racism' rather than 'United to bravely oppose racism forever'. We have often heard that racism is part of our human nature and therefore impossible to overcome. However, in the light of RC's basic assumptions, we know that this cannot be true. Only undischarged feelings of hopelessness (from early hurts) make us vulnerable to believing that it might be. In fact, racism can be ended. 'A next step for many of us is *thinking about being hopeful*, just trying to imagine what that would be' (T. Jackins 2001: 15 author's italic). Tim challenges us to dare to think about the possibility that oppressive patterns will become anachronisms, and that we can play a role in that process.

Other areas of work

Using RC outside of RC

Co-Counsellors have always been encouraged to use RC ideas freely and fully. From early on, they have taken what they found useful and used it to improve their lives: their relationships, their jobs and the functioning of the groups they belong to (e.g. Wolfe 1999). Some have taken what they've gained in RC into social change groups.

Delegations of Co-Counsellors attended the non-governmental forums for both the United Nations Fourth World Conference on Women in Beijing, China, in 1995, and the United Nations World Conference Against Racism in Durban, South Africa, in 2001. They led workshops in which participants were encouraged to speak out about their experiences, and in which members of different groups were assisted to listen to each other. These Co-Counsellors showed how Re-evaluation Counselling theory and practice can be used to work on internalised oppression and to take more effective action in the world. (The work of the RC project United to End Racism is described in Appendix 1.)

Children and families

One of the important and interesting areas explored by RC is that of families and children. Re-evaluation Counselling has no formal theory of child development, but does have considerable experience and knowledge. In RC we assume that a human being has an intelligent, well-functioning mind from some time before birth. 'Young people are fully human. They are not in training to "become fully human"' (Sazama 1999: 1).

We regard RC theory as fully applicable to babies and to children. This means that when babies cry, it has to do with recovery from distress. The distress may be due to present discomfort (hunger and so on), but very often the baby is also trying to unload distresses that happened hours, days or weeks earlier. Caretakers should first make sure there is no difficulty in the present moment. Then, if everything current is taken care of, they need to stay warmly present and allow the child to continue crying (Wipfler 1999).

Older children also need opportunities to use the discharge process. However, most adults find it difficult to listen attentively to children. Because our societies treat children as less important and less intelligent than adults, most adults have been trained to not pay good attention to children.

Adults who want to be effective RC counsellors for children always need to have many sessions themselves on how they were treated when young, before paying good attention to children will come easily. Children who have such adults available gradually overcome their distrust of adult attention, talk about and show themselves more fully (though not always in the same way adults do), and use the discharge process to recover from the ways they've been hurt (T. Jackins 2000b).

In conclusion

We hope that in this chapter we have given you an idea of how Re-evaluation Counselling theory and practice have emerged, and some of the more recent developments. Inevitably, there are aspects of Re-evaluation Counselling theory and practice that we have not been able to cover. Similarly, in earlier chapters, in which we enlisted help from others to broaden the book's perspective, we were able to cover only a fraction of the range of experiences of those who use this process. In particular, the experiences of Co-Counsellors outside of Ireland, England and the United States are not represented.

You can get a glimpse of the full scope of Re-evaluation Counselling, as well as more detailed treatment of the theory discussed in this chapter, by scanning the list of RC publications in Appendix 2 and visiting the RC websites http://www. rc.org and http:www.rationalisland.com.

We, Katie and Caroline, have very much enjoyed writing this book. It has meant a great deal to us to share this process which has been so important in our lives. We believe Re-evaluation Counselling's discovery of the significance of the discharge process and the exchange of attention has tremendous potential for accelerating human liberation. People everywhere seek freedom from both their individual distresses and systematically imposed hurts. We hope this information will be of assistance to them and to you.

Notes

1   Others have recognised that oppressive messages tend to be believed by, and to divide, the people at whom they are targeted. Franz Fanon (1967), the Algerian psychiatrist, wrote about how racist theories used to justify colonial rule were believed by the people who were misdescribed. Working in Brazil to try to undo the effects of colonialism, Paolo Freire described 'adjustment' and powerlessness as effects of oppression (Freire 1970: 4). More recently feminist psychologists have described how women's oppression becomes part of their view of themselves (Lerner 1984; Miller 1984).

2   As a result of this work, Edward Aguilar (1995) has described the RC Community as 'culturally competent' (he sees 'cultural competency' as a stage on a continuum from being destructive to other cultures to being able to move easily between them – cultural proficiency).

Appendix I

Working together to end racism

Healing from the damage caused by racism

Tim Jackins and others
(reprinted with permission from Rational Island Publishers)

Introduction

Groups of humans have been oppressed in a variety of ways throughout much of human history. Racism, one form of oppression, has existed for many centuries. Racism shapes and perpetuates the inequities of our societies and has become a part of our societal institutions.

Racism has become an integral part of our societies. It is not just an aberration of some small segment of the population. To end racism, policies must change, racist behavior must stop, the injustices from racism must be redressed, and all people must recover from the damage done to them by racism.

The main form of racism today is white racism – the one-way, institutionalized mistreatment of Africans, Indigenous peoples, Asians, Latin Americans, Arabs, and others and their descendants – people of color. Racism conditions people of European descent – white people – to act as agents of this mistreatment. All people are deeply hurt by racism. However, this system – of unequal access to the resources of society supported by violence, threats of violence, misinformation, lies, isolation, and greed – is directed at people targeted by racism and carried out by white people.

Again, one group is targeted by racist institutions and another is conditioned to act as the agent of racist oppression. This targeting has destroyed and damaged the lives of hundreds of millions of people, through slavery, apartheid, and racial discrimination in many forms. This conditioning has also deeply corrupted the lives of those who have been conditioned to act as agents of racism.

No group or individual should ever be targeted by racism. No characteristic, real or imagined, justifies racism. Those who have been targeted by racism comprise the vast majority of the human population. They are from a multitude of rich and vibrant cultures, cultures that have produced many of the best achievements of our species. There has never been, nor can there be, any rational justification of racism.

Although racism is aimed at particular sections of the population, it corrodes and corrupts the entire society, severely limiting society's progress. It also limits the progress of every individual in that society toward a full and meaningful life.

The work to end racist behavior undertaken by those who have been conditioned to be agents of racism is an important part of the work of United to End Racism. It is vital to the progress of all humans that those of us who have been conditioned by society to act as agents of racism make the ending of racism our goal. Racism has corrupted our lives, and it is in our interest, as well as in the interest of the rest of the world, that it be ended as quickly as possible.

The struggle to understand racism and to take action to eliminate it has progressed sufficiently that we can believe that racism will be ended in this century. People in many places have interrupted the worst manifestations of racism (such as slavery and apartheid) and have begun to secure broad agreement on policies to root out racism from many of society's institutions.

To end racism, it is vital that we remove racist policies from our institutions and ensure fair and just conditions of life for all. Accomplishing this will save future generations from the damage done to past generations. It is also vital to heal the damage done to individuals by racism. Healing this damage is not the same as ending racist policies. Only by healing the damage done to individuals can we be confident that racist attitudes and behaviors will not continue and that racist policies will not reappear in other guises.

To fully eliminate racism, we must heal three forms of damage.

The first form is the damage done to individuals targeted by racism – the hurts from being treated as inferior, denied basic material needs, denied a fair share of resources, demeaned, attacked, threatened with destruction, and much more. This damage is done to individuals through their contact with society's institutions and by the actions of individuals.

The second form is the damage to members of targeted groups that occurs from having 'internalized' racism. Racist attitudes can be so overpowering that they are absorbed by people targeted by racism. Racism shapes the way targeted people think and feel about themselves. It can make people mistreat themselves (and other members of their group) in ways that are similar to the mistreatment they have received from the agents of oppression. People end up mistreating themselves and each other. We call this 'internalized' racism.

The third form of damage is the corruption of the minds and spirits of those conditioned by society to act as the agents of racism (i.e., white people). No one is born an agent of racism. No one is born with a racist attitude. Anyone with a racist attitude has first been mistreated and misinformed. He or she has been conditioned to play that role.

Although individuals of the oppressor group are accorded more rights and better material lives than people in the oppressed group, their lives and minds are corrupted by racism. Racism damages everyone. It is in no one's real human interest.

All three forms of damage can be healed.

Even under the most severe racist oppression, people are able to move forward simply through the force of their own thinking and determination. However, unless they recover from the emotional hurts of racism, they continue to carry the effects of those hurts, and their thinking and behavior are affected by them. These hurts weigh heavily on each of them personally; the hurts also slow the work to bring about institutional change. Unhealed, these hurts from racism limit and damage everyone's abilities to think and work cooperatively and limit our capacity to end the other forms of oppression in our societies. They make the work and lives of those fighting institutionalized racism more difficult. In contrast, when people can heal from the effects of racism, they find it easier to work together, building strong alliances within their own liberation movement and between liberation movements.

If all racist behavior stopped immediately and racist policies were removed, the damage from past racism would not disappear. For those of us who are targeted, our feelings resulting from racism – feeling in danger, attacked, worthless, mistreated, ignored, doubting of ourselves – would continue to confuse us and erode our lives. For those of us trained by society to act as the agents of racism, the damage of having been conditioned to believe and act on the basis of racism (for example, feeling that one's own group is superior or feeling fear or discomfort around people targeted by racism) would also continue. It would confuse and corrupt both our thinking and behaviour and lead to the re-enactment of racist policies and actions.

The work of United to End Racism is to remove the damage done to individuals by racism. Both for people targeted by racism and for white people, healing from racism involves releasing the emotional tensions left from early hurtful experiences in our lives. When we are allowed and encouraged to tell fully the stories of how racism has affected us, with others listening and giving their full attention, we will begin to heal. When we are able not only to recount the facts of these stories, but also to allow ourselves to feel and show what it was like for us personally – feel and express the rage, grief, or terror – we become increasingly free of the damage of racism. All the emotional effects of racism can be healed if the person is given enough time, attention, and understanding.

Healing from mistreatment is not easy work. Many of us resist it, even though without this healing, the rage, grief, and terror from the past continue to affect us. We may feel that we have been able to persist in life only by numbing ourselves and holding inside how we were hurt. It may seem unbearable to look at and feel those hurts again – perhaps because for so long most of us had no opportunity to tell our stories. Some of us believe that we are no longer hurting since we continued to function in our lives, often very well, after the incidents of mistreatment. We mistakenly believe that we 'got over it'. Or we unawarely accept the idea that it is impossible to heal fully from racism.

From our work in UER, we now know that it is possible for us to get completely free of the damage done by racism. We know that all of us are capable of freeing ourselves. We know that the apparently unbearable feelings do not persist once the healing process begins. And we find that once we begin healing from these hurts, we can think more clearly and act more powerfully in our work to end racism. Healing from the effects of racism is not a substitute for organizing and taking action against institutional racism, but we in UER have found it to be a vital component of the work to end racism.

In the following sections of this pamphlet, not reprinted here, the nature of the damage caused by racism and the process to heal from it are described in more detail.

Copyright © 2001 The International Re-evaluation Counseling Communities.

United to End Racism (UER)

United to End Racism (UER) is a group of people of all ages and backgrounds, in many different countries, who are dedicated to eliminating racism in the world. We understand that eliminating racism is necessary for humankind to progress. We are committed to ending racism, and we support the efforts of other groups to accomplish this goal.

The main work of UER is to illuminate the damage done to individuals by racism and to undo this damage on an individual basis, using the resources and process of Re-evaluation Counseling. As people do this work, they become better able:

- to interrupt racism in their daily lives,
- to free themselves from all of racism's effects,
- to take leadership,
- to form deep relationships across racial lines,
- to remove racism from our societies' institutions, and
- to support the work of other individuals and organizations in ending racism.

UER also examines the racism in many of our societies' institutions and encourages its members to become actively aware of it and to find new ways of combating it. UER offers both an ongoing system of support that assists people to sustain their efforts to eliminate racism, and effective tools for eliminating racism that can be taught and used on a one-to-one basis.

Through its work, UER has developed a new and important understanding of racism and the relationships between racism and other oppressions. This understanding includes how racism and other oppressions are inflicted upon people, how they damage people, how this damage is passed from generation to generation, how people can resist such damage, and how people can recover from it. Our understanding is that racism is unintentionally internalised by those who have been targeted, operating within the targeted group to make that group's work to end racism more difficult. UER has also developed an understanding of the effects of racism on members of oppressor groups and how racist attitudes are installed on and persist in them.

Using this understanding of racism, UER has developed methods for undoing its damage. The work to recover from the damage of racism is done, in different ways, both by people who are members of groups targeted by racism and by people who are members of groups that play oppressive, racist roles.

In 2001, local RC Communities engaged in hundreds of projects in twenty countries to communicate about our work on ending racism. These projects included: workshops, house parties, public forums, film showings followed by discussions about racism, introductions to RC and UER, listening projects, report-backs from the UN World Conference Against Racism, and presentations at workshops and conferences held by other organizations.

Much of this work was done in preparation for and supportive to UER's sending a delegation to the UN World Conference Against Racism (WCAR), in Durban, South Africa, in August 2001. UER led workshops, panel speakouts, and support groups throughout the conference.

United to End Racism (UER) made many contacts at the WCAR, and with the help of these contacts the work of UER is continuing. UER activities since August 2001 include:

- UER participated in the Caribbean NGO (non-governmental organizations) Conference in Barbados.
- Workshops led by UER for NGO representatives in three cities in Nigeria, an AIDS organization in Johannesburg, a youth organization in Soweto, and for UNISA students in Durban, South Africa.
- Workshops have been held in Colombia, Ecuador, Peru, and Chile.
- UER led a series of workshops for women farmworkers in southern California, USA.
- Co-Counseling classes have started for NGO representatives in Durban and Capetown, South Africa, and Falkirk, Scotland.
- UER also participated in the U.S. NGO Conference 'Building a Racial Justice Vision in the Post-Durban, Post 9/11 Era.'

Additional follow-up UER workshops are planned for Africa, South America, northern Europe, and the United States.

Re-evaluation Counselling publications

- *The Human Side of Human Beings: The Theory of Re-evaluation Counseling* (Harvey Jackins 1965, revised 2001). The first written introduction to Re-evaluation Counselling.
- *Fundamentals of Co-Counseling Manual, for beginning classes in Re-evaluation Counseling* (Harvey Jackins, 3rd edn, 1982). A simply written how-to-do-it manual.
- *The Human Situation* (Harvey Jackins, 1973). An early collection of writings on Re-evaluation Counselling.
- *The List: 'Everything I know about Re-evaluation Counseling (and the world) until now'* (Harvey Jackins, 2nd edn, 1997).
- *Rough Notes from Liberation I and II* (Harvey Jackins and others 1976). Transcript of a workshop for Co-Counsellors interested in liberation movements.
- 'The Art of Listening' (Harvey Jackins 1981b). A succinct review of the interactions involved in paying attention.
- 'The Distinctive Characteristics of Re-evaluation Counseling' (Harvey Jackins 1973a). What differentiates Re-evaluation Counselling from humanistic psychologies.
- *How 'Re-evaluation Counseling' Began* (Harvey Jackins 1994).
- *Letter to a Respected Psychiatrist* (Harvey Jackins 1973d).
- *Guidelines for the Re-evaluation Counseling Communities* (Re-evaluation Counseling 2002).
- *How to Begin 'Re-evaluation Counseling'* (Rational Island Publishers 1996). A convenient pocket-size booklet with simple instructions.
- *Internalized Racism* (Suzanne Lipsky 1987). An essay on the internalisation of racist oppression.
- *The Postulates of Re-evaluation Counseling* (Harvey Jackins 1990). The axiomatic foundations of Re-evaluation Counselling theory.
- *What's Wrong with the 'Mental Health' System and What Can Be Done about It*. A draft policy prepared for the Re-evaluation Counseling Communities.
- *Present Time*. The quarterly journal of Re-evaluation Counselling.

• *Recovery and Re-emergence.* An RC journal for those interested in 'mental health' issues.

For a complete list of publications about Re-evaluation Counselling see www. rationalisland.com.

How to contact Re-evaluation Counselling

The International Re-evaluation Counseling Communities
719 Second Avenue North
Seattle, Washington 98109, USA
Email: ircc@rc.org
Home page: http://www.rc.org/
Voice: +1 206 284 0311
Fax: +1 206 284 8429

Contact the authors at www.KauffmanNew.com

References

Aguilar, E. (1995) *Re-evaluation Counseling: A 'Culturally Competent' Model for Social Liberation*, Seattle, WA: Rational Island Publishers.

Barham, P. and Hayward, R. (1995) *Relocating Madness: From the Mental Patient to the Person*, London: Free Association.

Breggin, P. R. (1993) *Toxic Psychiatry*, London: HarperCollins.

Breuer, J. and Freud, S. (1955) *Studies in Hysteria*, Boston, MA: Beacon Press.

Bronstein, P. (1984) 'Promoting Healthy Emotional Development in Children', *Journal of Primary Prevention*, 5, 2: 92–110.

—— (1986) 'Re-evaluation Counseling: A Self-Help Model for Recovery from Emotional Distress', in E. D. Rothman and E. Cole (eds) *A Woman's Recovery from the Trauma of War*, New York: Haworth.

Brown, G. (1999) *Why Lead in RC?* Seattle, WA: Rational Island Publishers.

Digby, A. (1985) 'Moral Treatment at the Retreat', in *The Anatomy of Madness: Essays in the History of Psychiatry*, Vol. II, *Institutions and Society*, eds W. F. Bynum, R. Porter and M. Shepherd, London: Tavistock.

Dobson, K. S. (ed.) (2000) *Handbook of Cognitive-Behavioral Therapies*, 2nd edn, New York: Guilford Press.

Fanon, F. (1967) *The Wretched of the Earth*, Harmondsworth: Penguin.

Freire, P. (1970) *Pedagogy of the Oppressed*, New York: Continuum.

Freud, S. (1957) 'Thoughts for the Times on War and Death' (1915), *Standard Edition*, Vol. XIV, London: Hogarth Press.

—— (1962) 'The Aetiology of Hysteria' (1896), *Standard Edition*, Vol. III, London: Hogarth Press.

Gardner, H. (1993) *Frames of Mind: The Theory of Multiple Intelligences*, London: Fontana.

Gregory, R. (1987) *The Oxford Companion to the Mind*, Oxford: Oxford University Press.

House, R. and Totton, N. (eds) (1997) *Implausible Professions: Arguments for Pluralism and Autonomy in Psychotherapy and Counselling*, Ross-on-Wye: PCCS Books.

Irwin, J., Jackins, H. and Kreiner, C. (1992) *The Liberation of Men*, Seattle, WA: Rational Island Publishers.

Jackins, H. (1965) *The Human Side of Human Beings*, Seattle: Rational Island Publishers.

—— (1972) Unpublished transcript, meeting in Seattle, WA: October.

—— (1973a) 'The Distinctive Characteristics of Re-evaluation Counseling', in *The Human Situation*, Seattle, WA: Rational Island Publishers.

—— (1973b) 'Who's in Charge?', in *The Human Situation*, Seattle, WA: Rational Island Publishers.

—— (1973c) 'The Complete Appreciation of Oneself', in *The Human Situation*, Seattle, WA: Rational Island Publishers.

Jackins, H. (1973d) 'Letter to a respected Psychiatrist', in *The Human Situation*, Seattle, WA: Rational Island Publishers.

—— (1978a) 'Powerlessness is a Fraud', in *The Upward Trend*, Seattle, WA: Rational Island Publishers.

—— (1978b) 'The Rational Needs of Human Beings', in *The Upward Trend*, Seattle, WA: Rational Island Publishers.

—— (1978c) 'Counseling the Way It Should Have Been Done All the Time', in *The Upward Trend*, Seattle, WA: Rational Island Publishers.

—— (1978d) 'Don't Stop at the Permissive Counseling Level', in *The Upward Trend*, Seattle, WA: Rational Island Publishers.

—— (1978e) 'The Nature of Theory', in *The Upward Trend*, Seattle, WA: Rational Island Publishers.

—— (1981a) 'Courage', in *The Benign Reality*, Seattle, WA: Rational Island Publishers.

—— (1981b) 'The Art of Listening', in *The Benign Reality*, Seattle, WA: Rational Island Publishers.

—— (1981c) 'A Rational Theory of Sexuality', in *The Benign Reality*, Seattle, WA: Rational Island Publishers.

—— (1981d) 'The Fundamentals of Co-Counseling', in *The Benign Reality*, Seattle, WA: Rational Island Publishers.

—— (1983a) 'The Counselor as Bagpiper', in *The Reclaiming of Power*, Seattle, WA: Rational Island Publishers.

—— (1983b) 'The "Belief" System of Re-evaluation Counseling', in *The Reclaiming of Power*, Seattle, WA: Rational Island Publishers.

—— (1985) 'Understanding the "Blue Pages" and the "No Socializing" Principle', in *The Rest of Our Lives*, Seattle, WA: Rational Island Publishers.

—— (1987) *The Enjoyment of Leadership*, Seattle, WA: Rational Island Publishers.

—— (1990) *The Postulates of Re-evaluation Counselling*, Seattle, WA: Rational Island Publishers.

—— (1992) 'Advanced Re-emergence', in *A Better World*, Seattle, WA: Rational Island Publishers.

—— (1993a) *Quotes*, Seattle, WA: Rational Island Publishers.

—— (1993b) 'Another Step Towards More Skilful Counseling', in *The Kind, Friendly Universe*, Seattle, WA: Rational Island Publishers.

—— (1993c) 'A Year of Continental and World Conferences', in *The Kind, Friendly Universe*, Seattle, WA: Rational Island Publishers.

—— (1993d) 'Being an Ally', in *The Kind, Friendly Universe*, Seattle, WA: Rational Island Publishers.

—— (1994) *How 'Re-evaluation Counseling' Began*, Seattle, WA: Rational Island Publishers.

—— (1997) *The List*, Seattle, WA: Rational Island Publishers.

—— (2003) 'The Way Important Theory Evolves', *Present Time*, 35, 2: 5.

Jackins, H. and others (1976) *Rough Notes from Liberation I and II*, Seattle, WA: Rational Island Publishers.

Jackins, H. and others (1999) *The Human Male: A Men's Liberation Draft Policy*, Seattle, WA: Rational Island Publishers.

Jackins, T. (2000a) 'Our Choice Against Racism', *Present Time*, 32, 3: 27–8.

—— (2000b) *How Parents Can Counsel their Children*, Seattle, WA: Rational Island Publishers.

—— (2001) 'Hope', *Present Time*, 33, 1: 15.

—— (2002) 'Close, Caring Contact', *Present Time*, 34, 4: 3.

—— (2003) 'Our Relationships with Each Other', *Present Time*, 35, 1: 25.

Lerner, H. (1984) 'Special Issues for Women in Psychotherapy', in P. Rieker and E. Carmen (eds) *The Gender Gap in Psychotherapy*, New York: Plenum Press.

Lieberman, E. J. (1997) 'The Evolution of Psychotherapy since Freud', *Psychiatric Times*, 14, 4. Online. Available http://www.ottorank.com/evolution.htm (17 September 2003).

Lipsky, S. (1987) *Internalised Racism*, Seattle, WA: Rational Island Publishers.

Malinowski, B. (1960) *Sex and Repression in Savage Society*, London: Routledge and Kegan Paul.

Maslow, A. (1968) *Towards a Psychology of Being*, New York: D. Van Nostrand.

—— (1973) *The Farther Reaches of Human Nature.* Harmondsworth: Penguin.

Mason, M. (2002) 'Inclusion', *Present Time*, 34, 4: 70–1.

Miller, J. B. (1984) *Towards a New Psychology of Women*, Harmondsworth: Penguin.

New, C. (1996) *Agency, Health and Social Survival: The Ecopolitics of Rival Psychologies*, London: Taylor and Francis.

Palmer, S., Dainow, S. and Milner, P. (1996) *The BAC Counselling Reader*, London: Sage with British Association for Counselling.

Perls, F. S. (1972) 'Four Lectures', in J. Fagan and I. Shepherd (eds) *Gestalt Therapy Now.* Harmondsworth: Penguin.

Personal Counselors (1962) *Fundamentals of Co-Counseling Manual*, Seattle, WA: Rational Island Publishers.

Ramachandran, V. S. and Blakeslee, S. (1998) *Phantoms in the Brain: Human Nature and the Architecture of the Mind*, London: Fourth Estate.

Read, J. (2001) *Thinking about a drug-free future for Mental Health Services*, http://www.critpsynet.freeuk.com/Read.htm (14 September 2003).

Re-evaluation Counseling (1991) *What is Wrong with the 'Mental Health' System and What Can Be Done about It: A Draft Policy*, Seattle, WA: Rational Island Publishers.

—— (2002) *Guidelines of the Re-evaluation Counseling Communities*, Seattle, WA: Rational Island Publishers.

Roby, P. (1998) 'Creating a Just World: Leadership for the Twenty-First Century', *Social Problems*, 45, 1: 1–20.

Rogers, C. (1990) 'The Necessary and Sufficient Conditions of Therapeutic Personality Change', in *The Carl Rogers Reader*, London: Constable.

Rowan, J. (1976) *Ordinary Ectasy: Humanistic Psychology in Action*, London: Routledge.

Ruth, S. (1998) 'Middle Class Liberation', *Our True Selves*, 1: 1.

Rycroft, C. (1984) 'A Case of Hysteria', *New York Review*, 12 April.

Sazama, J. (1999) *Understanding and Supporting Young People*, Seattle, WA: Rational Island Publishers.

Scheff, T. J. (1972) 'Re-evaluation Counseling: Social Implications', *Journal of Humanistic Psychology*, 12, 1: 58–71.

Somers, B. (1972) 'Re-evaluation Therapy: Theoretical Framework', *Journal of Humanistic Psychology*, 12, 1: 42–57.

Stevens, A. (1998) *An Intelligent Person's Guide to Psychotherapy*, London: Duckworth.

Wachtel, P. L. (1977) *Psychoanalysis and Behavior Therapy*, New York: Basic Books.

Warner, R. (1985) *Recovery from Schizophrenia: Psychiatry and Political Economy*, London: Routledge.

Wipfler, P. (1999) *Listening Effectively to Children*, Seattle, WA: Rational Island Publishers.

Wolfe, R. B. (1999) 'Listening to Children: A New Approach to Parent Support, Education and Empowerment', *Family Science Review*, 12, 4: 275–93.

Index

addictions 50, 80; addictive behaviours 49,
   92
advice: not helpful in counselling 15, 30,
   58, 63, 128
adult(s) 11, 62; at young people's
   workshop 67
African American 68, 98, 103; *see also*
   black people
ageism 10, 11, 92
agents of oppression 74, 139
agreements in counselling 55–7; *see also*
   Guidelines
alcohol 57; alcoholism 90
ally, allies to oppressed groups 90, 93, 140
Alternate International Reference Person
   3, 132
anger, angry 1, 22, 26, 30, 34, 76, 108;
   discharge of 1, 43, 47, 58, 92, 108, 117
antidepressants 53, 119
anti-Semitism 11, 38; *see also* anti-Jewish
   oppression
anxiety 123
anti-Jewish oppression 84
appreciation 15–16, 65, 70, 140–1; *see
   also* self-appreciation
Arabs 93
Area Reference People 131
Areas, Co-Counselling 131, 132
art, artists 62, 112
Asians 74
attention 3, 11, 12, 13, 52–4; off distress
   137; free 58; giving and receiving 10,
   12, 52, 55, 57; on reality 62;
awareness 20, 34, 62

babies 9, 45, 60, 94–7, 142
bagpiper analogy 61

behavioural approaches 118, 123–125
benign nature of world, benign reality 10,
   70, 137
biopsychiatry 118, 119
birth 15, 45, 96
black people 14, 49, 81–2, 86, 103; black
   women 14, 81; *see also* African
   American
blame, blaming 33
blue-collar 76; *see also* working-class
boys 44, 45, 47, 53, 58, 88; oppression of
   77
brain research 8

capitalist countries 32
catharsis 120
Catholic(s) 88, 90, 93
caucus 2
chemical imbalance 38
Chicanos/as 74
child development 142
childhood: 49, 98
children 47, 52, 54, 89, 142; *see also*
   young people
chronic pattern(s) *see* distress patterns,
   distress recordings
class: 69, 76, 112
classism 11, 34, 69, 74, 76, 78–81
client 1, 13; role of 12, 55, 57, 59, 60, 89
closeness 8, 52, 63, 68, 121, 137, 138;
   natural state 45; physical 64, 92
Co-Counselling class(es) 3, 6, 12; *see also*
   Fundamentals class(es)
Co-Counselling International (CCI) 129
Co-Counselling 1–2; development 41–2;
   process 52–72; taking turns 12, 55, 69;
   see also Co-Counselling relationships

Co-Counselling relationships 56, 60, 92, 100–1; examples of 68–9, 71–2, 112–5
cognitive behaviour therapy (CBT) 124
Complete Appreciation of Oneself, The 15
confidence in counselling 1, 60, 67
connection 8, 35, 52, 63, 138; natural state 45
conditioning 19, 44, 53, 123, 124
confidentiality 56, 123; *see also* agreements
consensus 132
contact 10, 45, 121; eye 12; physical 64
contradict, contradiction 58, 59–61, 122–3, 124, 127; closeness as 63–4; 69, 136; examples 81, 100; of hurts from oppression 75; reality as 62, 139
co-operative nature of humans, co-operation 8–9, 125, 126;
counsellor, counselling 1; *see also* counsellor role, Co-Counselling
Co-Counselling 1, 2, 52–72; relationships 56, 60, 68–9, 64, 71–2, 92, 100–1, 112–5; taking turns 12, 55, 69
counsellor role 1, 12, 55, 57– 61, 89
criticism 70
crying: alone 48, 49, 98; in babies 96–7; disapproved of for males 1, 44, 23, 91; as discharge of grief 1, 42, 44; examples 17, 22, 41, 45–8, 70, 97, 104; with physical contact 64
culture, cultural: misinformation 11, 53; patterns 32; traditions 93;

Daire 5, 16, 25, 39, 48, 88
death 71; near-death experience 17
decision 66, 68, 124; not to be restimulated 135
deductive structure of Re-evaluation Counselling theory 135
delight, counsellor's attitude of 68, 71, 104–5, 126
depression 91, 107
despair 10, 100; and Gay oppression 85
diagnosis(es) 119
directions, in counselling 66, 104
disabled people's oppression 78, 82–3
discharge 1, 41–51; access to 44, 58, 61–2; assisting client to 58; in babies 95–7; gender and 91; health and 93; social discouragement of 44, 53–4;
disconnection, feelings of 45
discrimination: *see* oppression

distress 1, 117; contagious 11; early 11, 30, 50, 61–2, 127; from oppression 74, 103, 126; rehearsal of 30, 106; *see also* distress patterns, distress recordings
distress patterns: acting outside 30, 124; chronic 29, 30, 36, 38, 113, 126, 127, 136, 137; intermittent, 29, 36, 38, 93. 136; pattern not person 31, 33–4, 38, 39–40, 126–7; socially acceptable 32; violent 103–11
distress recordings 21–24, 29–31, 32; accumulation of 23; chronic 30–1; taking more powerful role in 31
draft policies 131, 139
drugs, RC policy about 57, 119

Ebony 6, 14, 27, 36, 48, 54, 81
electro-convulsive therapy (ECT) 41, 104
embarrassment, discharge of 43, 63
Emma 4, 17, 26, 35, 47, 70, 78, 82
emotion: *see* fear, grief, anger, etc.; feelings, discharge
England, English 127
equal time: as counsellor and client, 57, 69 *see also* peers
exchange of attention: *see* attention

fantasies, fantasising 121
fear, discharge of 42, 64, 91; *see also* terror
feelings 10, 43, 63; bad 26, 28, 46, 49–51, 59; feeling, 32, 36, 47, 62–3 (*see also* numbness); unwise to act on 21, 34, 65, 97
female 53, 64, 69, 73, 77, 81; *see also* woman
flexibility, flexible intelligence 19–20, 22–3
free associations 122
Freud, Sigmund 119–122
frozen needs 63–4
functioning 8, 11, 21, 49, 66, 106, 124, 125, 126; despite bad feelings 98, 99–100; dominated by chronic patterns 30–1
Fundamentals of Co-Counselling Manual, The 2, 130
Fundamentals, Fundamentals class(es) 2, 3, 14, 16, 56, 62

Gay, gay/lesbian/bisexual, 5, 46
Gay oppression 11, 85–6

gender(s) 3, 10, 85, 88
Gestalt 126
Gillian 4, 15, 26, 36, 47, 55, 67, 78
girls 44, 45, 47, 53, 58, 77, 79, 88
God 53, 90
goodness, inherent human 7, 8, 15, 16, 33, 92
grief, discharge of 17, 23, 26, 48
Guidelines of the Re-evaluation Counselling Communities 55, 111, 131
guilt 141

Harvey Jackins, *see* Jackins
healing 41; *see also* recovery
heterosexual 46 86; as allies to Gays 85
homosexual: *see* Gay, Lesbian
hope, hopeful, hopefulness 10, 140–1
How Re-evaluation Counselling Began 41
human nature, inherent 7–18, 98, 125
Human Side of Human Beings, The 2, 19, 130
Human Situation, The 2
humanistic psychology 125, 128
hurt(s) 7, 10–11, 15, 33, 77; accumulated 31, 62; how we get hurt, 11; from oppression 2, 74–89
hypnosis 120

inclusion 138
Indigenous people 74
individual leadership 132
inductive structure 135
infantile sexuality 121
infants 45; *see also* babies
intelligence: definition 7–8, 19; flexibility 20; when hurting 21, 23, 24, 25, 30–1; recovery as aim 19, 74, 103;
intermittent pattern: *see* distress pattern
internalised oppression 77, 78, 80, 139, 142
International Liberation Reference Person 132
International Reference Person 3, 111, 132
interpret, interpretations 58, 122
Irish, 88, 127
Irwin 77
isolation 28, 60, 45, 137, 138

Jackins, Harvey vii, 1, 2, 7, 9, 18, 19, 29, 30, 41, 43, 52, 64, 73, 77, 124, 125, 126, 130, 131, 132, 133, 134, 135, 136, 137, 138, 140

Jackins, Tim, 2, 137, 138, 141
Jenny 6, 15, 28, 39, 49, 70, 89
Jews, Jewish 38, 49, 84, 90, 139
justice 8

Kerry 5, 14, 28, 38, 55, 84

Latinos/as 74
laughter, laughing 1, 2, 15, 42, 43, 44, 49;
leadership 3, 65–66, 81, 98, 129, 132, 133
Lebanese 93
Lesbian(s) 68, 74, 85
Liberation Reference Persons 132
List, The 67
logic, acting on, 65, 69
love 9, 15, 34, 63, 92, 121

madness 118, 119
male 53, 64, 69, 73, 77; *see also* men
Mansour 90
Maslow 125
medical model 118–119
memory, memories 19, 67; recovery of 67; storage 20–1
men 3, 46, 77; oppression of 77, 78; *see also* boys
mental 'illness', mentally 'ill' 15, 118–119
mental health oppression 83–4
'mental health' system 2, 90, 116
mental patient(s) 16
middle-class 76, 87; oppression of, 87–8, 93, 94, 138, 139
mini-sessions 12
Muslim 64

nature, human; *see* human nature
needs, meeting 10, 11, 57, 63–4, 125, 126
Neil 5, 13, 27, 36, 45, 54, 67, 78, 85
'nervous breakdown' 50
nervous system 8
no socializing 56, 64, 123, 129
Northern Irish, Northern Ireland 5, 14
numb, numbness 15, 32–3, 62, 67, 87, 92, 121

occlusion, occluded incidents 50, 120
Oedipus 121
one-point programme of the Re-evaluation Counselling Communities 103, 131
oppression, 73–89, 129, 139–141; definition of 11, 74; discharging 75, 76;

internalized 77; as source of hurt 11, 64, 73
oppressed role 69, 74, 75, 76, 89, 140
oppressor role 74, 75, 76, 87, 89, 140
oppressed groups 3, 74
oppressive societies 126, 138, 140
owning-class 69, 138, 139

parents, parenting 11, 46, 58, 94–7, 139
patterns, *see* distress patterns
peers, peer counselling, 57, 69, 98
people of colour 93
Perls, Fritz 125, 126
Personal Counsellors, Inc. 2, 42, 130
personality 30
pharmaceutical industry 118
phobias 123
playgroup, RC 47–8
policies, always draft, 133, 134
poor people, poverty 32, 81, 139
Postulates of Re-evaluation Counselling 135
power, powerful 9, 114
powerlessness 32; contradicting 59; feeling of 12, 23, 28
pre-natal 45
Present Time 2, 67, 137
Protestants, Protestantism 6, 138
pseudo reality 136; *see also* reality
psychiatrists, 16, 41, 118 119
psychoanalysis 119–122, 125, 128
psychologists 16
psychotherapy, vii
psychotic 119
publication(s) 131

Rachael 6, 15, 28, 38, 49, 55, 69, 84
racism 10, 14, 32, 34, 102–3
rage, raging 58, 104–5; *see also* anger
rational emotive behaviour therapy 124
RC: *see* Re-evaluation Counselling
RC Community: *see* Re-evaluation Counselling Communities
RC teachers 131
reality 59; attention on reality 62, 69, 75, 98; pseudo-reality 136
recovery 23, 41–51, 98
recovery process 41–51, 53
re-evaluation 43, 48, 75, 92, 122, 127
Re-evaluation Counselling 2, 90; distinctiveness of 117; key features 117–8

Re-evaluation Counselling Communities 3, 74, 91,123, 130, 132, 138, 143
Reference Person 134; *see* Area, Regional, International, and International Liberation Reference Person(s)
Regional Reference People 132
relationships 123; as contradiction 63, Co-Counselling relationships 56, 60, 64, 68, 71, 92; and frozen needs 63–4
religion 34, 37; religious frameworks 8
responsible, responsibility 9, 32, 33
restimulation 22, 23, 25–8, 37, 45, 58, 75–6, 123; deciding against 128, 135–136
rigid behaviour, rigidities 59, 93
Roby, Pam 78
Rogers, Carl 126, 127

safety 49, 58, 59, 64, 75, 123, 127, 128
schizophrenic 107, 126
science 134
self-appreciation 15, 39
self-disclosure 128
session, Co-Counselling 12, 65; examples 37, 39, 69, 70, 100, 104–5; value of 49, 60
sexism 11, 34, 73, 74, 77, 92
sexual abuse 121
sexual distress 121–122
sexuality 121
shake, shaking 41, 42, 44, 46, 91
Shisk, Diane, 3
social change 141
social structure 126, 139
society 141; *see also* oppressive society
socializing, no socializing policy 56, 69
suicide 100, 110
support group(s) 76, 87, 92, 94, 96, 131

taking turns 2, 55; *see also* Co-Counselling
talk, talking, non-repetitive talking 2, 43
tantrum 43, 44, 49
techniques 60
terror 42, 45, 50; *see also* fear
theory: development of 42–3, 130, 133, 134–7, 139; summary of 1–2
transference 122, 123
trauma 50

tremble, trembling 1, 42; *see also*
    shaking
true self 15, 29, 33; distinct from
    recordings 34, 38, 39; (*see also* distress
    pattern)
trust 1

unconditional positive regard 126
unconscious 120
United Nations World Conference Against
    Racism 141
United Nations World Conference on
    Women 141
United States 2, 39, 90, 142
United to End Racism (UER) 77, 141

validate, validation 31, 65, 70

victim 31, 34, 69; refusing role of 65–6,
    84; victimisation 102

white people 86
white racism: *see* racism
women 3, 77, 139
working-class 36, 76, 88, 111, 112–4;
    oppression of 78–81, 90, 93, 94
workshop(s) 56, 131
world conference, of RC 132

yawn, yawning 1, 43, 44, 47, 53
young people 8, 19, 28, 53, 139;
    oppression of 11, 32, 60, 78, 87, 88–9;
    workshops for 67;

zest 1, 9